About the Auth...

Dorothy Chitty is a gifted medium who has changed many people's lives. Born in Birmingham, England, she has been able to communicate with the spirit world for as long as she can remember. She has always known that she is meant to use her psychic abilities to help others.

For the last thirty years Dorothy has given spiritual readings to clients to help them find answers and clarity where there is confusion, loss or worry. As a result she has become one of the most sought-after psychic experts in the country, with celebrities, royalty, film stars and politicians all calling on her for guidance, along with her everyday clients. Dorothy's work takes her all over the world, although most of her clients are based in the UK or USA.

Dorothy firmly believes that we should all try to communicate better with our own angels and guides as they are always trying to help us make the best decisions in our lives and to find love, happiness and success in what we do. When she conducts a reading, she receives information from our guides and not just from her own. If we learn to listen to our guides then we will be able to hear the answers to our questions too. This is why Dorothy also runs a variety of spiritual awareness seminars and workshops throughout the year.

Dorothy has three grown-up children and lives with her husband in Devon.

To find out more about Dorothy and the incredible work she does please visit www.dorothychitty.co.uk.

An Angel
set me free

By the same author
Are You Psychic?

An Angel
set me free

And other incredible true
stories of the afterlife

Dorothy Chitty

HarperElement
An Imprint of HarperCollins*Publishers*
77–85 Fulham Palace Road,
Hammersmith, London W6 8JB

www.harpercollins.co.uk

and *HarperElement* are trademarks of
HarperCollins*Publishers* Ltd

First published by HarperElement 2009

1 3 5 7 9 10 8 6 4 2

© Dorothy Chitty 2009

Dorothy Chitty asserts the moral right to be
identified as the author of this work

Edited by Gill Paul

A catalogue record of this book is
available from the British Library

ISBN 978-0-00-731901-5

Printed and bound in Great Britain by
Clays Ltd, St Ives plc

FSC is a non-profit international organisation established to promote the
responsible management of the world's forests. Products carrying the FSC
label are independently certified to assure consumers that they come
from forests that are managed to meet the social, economic and
ecological needs of present and future generations.

Find out more about HarperCollins and the environment at
www.harpercollins.co.uk/green

I dedicate this book to five of my angels –
my grandchildren Thomas, Byron, Harrison,
Eliot and India.

Contents

Preface

Angels are always around us. In fact, they are watching over you right now as you read this book. Whether you believe in them or not, they have been guiding you since the day you were born and chances are they have helped you out of umpteen scrapes you're not even aware of. That's what they do.

Many people consult me to find out about the spirit world after they have lost a loved one, wanting to understand more about where their father, mother, grandparent, sibling, child or partner has gone and what they are doing now. Other people come to me when something extraordinary has happened to them that can't be explained by the laws of nature and science. Or they might turn up on my doorstep when they have a big life decision to make and they need some guidance. Whatever the question, I close my eyes and pray and the spirits come to me bringing comfort and answers for the person across the room.

However, in this book I want to explain that to a certain extent we can all do this for ourselves by learning to watch, listen, ask and be aware. I run seminars in which I teach people how to open up to the spirit world, but here I decided to tell you some stories about angels helping people on earth in order to describe how the process works. Once you understand this, you can ask the angels for help yourself at any time.

And it's important to ask. Sure, angels will help you when you haven't asked, even if you think the whole concept is fanciful. But once you learn how to be in touch with spirit, your life will be immeasurably enriched in all sorts of ways.

Angels can help with practical life decisions such as which house to buy and which partner to marry. They can warn us about danger and sometimes even rescue us if we ignore the warning. They can heal sickness and comfort the bereaved. I've got a wide range of stories in this book, from the funny (such as the woman whose skirt was tucked in her knickers as she walked through Reading train station) to the terrifying (the soldier in Iraq whose armoured vehicle narrowly avoided being blown up by a roadside bomb).

In most (but not all) of the stories, the people concerned were in some way following the wrong path in life. They'd got side-tracked and were trapped in situations that weren't doing them any good. Maybe they were in the wrong career, or had become too obsessed with wealth and status; some people had slipped into careless disregard for their own safety or that of others; a few got bogged down by grief and depression: there are dozens of ways in which we get stuck in life. It's happened to me as well, as I'll explain in chapter 1. No one's immune.

The point is that listening to angels can get you back on track and release you from anxiety about the future. All will be well, for you and everyone you care about, when you lead a spiritually aware life. That doesn't need to mean worship in a church, but simply treating others (including animals) as you would like to be treated your-self.

Angels will help you to make your life the best it can possibly be. Listen to them, and they will set you free.

An Angel
set me free

Chapter 1

The Angels in My Life

'Come on, Dolly Daydream,' Dad used to say to me at least twenty times a day, when he was trying to get me to come to the table for tea, or put my nightie on for bed. 'You're in a world of your own.'

He was right – I was. I didn't realise at that stage that my world was different from other people's. I just knew that there were always characters around me who weren't members of our family, right from when I was a small child in my cot. It was a big old wooden cot, and one of my earliest memories is of five people bending over it and looking at me lovingly. Of course I couldn't count at that age, but somehow I knew in my head that there were five. They looked so nice that it didn't occur to me to be scared. I felt very safe and protected with them there and it wasn't until I was much older that I looked back and realised they were angels, and that no one else in the house could see them.

I had a brother who was six years older than me and a sister who was three years older, but I was a very solitary child, perfectly content with my own company – and that of the angels who surrounded me. Occasionally I would surprise adults with the things I came out with. As Mum and I walked along the road one day, I pointed to a woman on the other side.

'That lady is going to die soon,' I said.

'Goodness!' Mum exclaimed. 'What makes you say that?' I was only three or four, so a bit young to know about death.

I frowned. 'I just know.'

Sure enough, the lady did pass away shortly afterwards and I heard the adults saying she had died of duck egg poisoning. It made me too scared to eat duck eggs, and to this day I always avoid them!

I started in the local Catholic school at the age of five, and we had an assembly in the church every morning. A kind man in a rough-textured brown suit used to sit next to me and explain what the Latin sermon was about and I listened, fascinated by the beauty of it all. He never told me his name but in my child's brain I assumed that he was God, and that's how I came to think of him. Woe betide me, though, when I mentioned to one of the nuns that 'God' had been speaking to me. I soon learned not to refer to my brown-suited friend any more because they were very liberal in their use of the strap at that school, particularly for what they thought of as blasphemy.

Sometimes the man in the brown suit took me out of school to a nearby park. I loved riding on the big wooden roundabout but was too little to climb up myself, so he lifted me up to stand on the platform and span it around. We had to cross several busy roads to get there but I never came to any harm. One day I stopped in front of the sweet shop window to peer in at all the tempting goodies on display. Suddenly I realised I couldn't see the reflection of my friend, although I could see myself clearly.

'That's right,' he said, reading my mind. 'Not everyone can see me.'

Gradually I learned not to mention him to anyone at school because I got teased so much. 'She's the one who talks to God,' the other girls would mock. They wouldn't let me join in their games in the playground because I was thought of as a kind of oddball, an outsider.

I still hadn't learned to censor myself and sometimes I passed on things I had been told by an angel. One day a girl called Carol was crying. I was always drawn to anyone who was sad, so I went over to her. I knew her father had been injured in the war and that there was something wrong with his lungs, and I also knew that he wasn't going to live much longer.

'Everyone says he will be all right,' Carol sniffed through her tears.

'No, he won't,' I told her matter-of-factly.

She gasped. 'You're being horrible!'

'But he'll be all right once he dies,' I said, 'because he will be an angel and he'll be with you all the time then.'

She asked me about angels – what they look like and how you talk to them and seemed reassured by my answers, that you can't always see them but that they talk to you in your head. I told her to tell her daddy that she loved him because I could sense she was a little scared of him and had never actually said those words before, and she promised she would.

Not long afterwards, Carol's father passed away and she and I became very close friends for the rest of our time at that school. But I was beginning to realise that it is better not to tell people bad news most of the time. You can help a lot more by passing on nice messages rather than negative ones.

When I was young, Mum and Dad seemed quite accepting when I told them I talked to God and saw angels. 'You're a very lucky girl,' Dad said once. But I think the whole family was disturbed when I started passing on messages from my Uncle Charlie, who committed suicide by sticking his head in the gas oven when I was ten. (He wasn't a proper uncle, but a family friend we knew by that name.)

When Charlie first appeared to me, his tongue was sticking out and his face was contorted just as it must have been in the moment of death, but I wasn't scared for one moment. It felt totally normal. Charlie told me that he had killed himself because he'd found out that his new wife was leaving him for someone else and he just couldn't face life without her, but he wanted the rest of the family to know that he was fine now. He came back with love rather than hatred or resentment. He was a gentle man, a caring soul.

We often went for Sunday lunch at the home of Charlie's mother, who we called Granny Watts, and Charlie would give me messages to pass on while we were sitting over our roast. I think it made the grown-ups round the table very uncomfortable.

Things really flared up, though, after a nun at school accused me of cheating. I had written something that my brown-suited friend 'God' told me was the correct answer to a question. After the nun read it, she charged over and hit me across the head.

'Where have you copied this from?' she demanded. 'These words are too adult, these are not your words.'

'No,' I said, 'they're God's words.'

The nun looked down at me with her podgy face close to mine. 'Read my lips,' she snarled. 'You cannot hear God. It is not possible.'

I got a good hiding that day, and it was reported to my parents that I was cheating at my schoolwork and disrupting the class with my cheeky answers when challenged. Next thing I knew I was being marched off for an appointment with a psychiatrist.

The psychiatrist was an austere man with dark hair and glasses, who kept firing questions at me and scribbling notes on his pad. I looked down and there, in front of his desk, was a little blond boy who told me his name was Peter. He was a very pretty-looking child and seemed to have a glow about him. He told me the psychiatrist was his father. He had died of leukaemia the previous year and mentioned that his dad had put a little teddy in his coffin. 'Tell my daddy I'm here,' he said, so I did.

'What on earth are you talking about?' the psychiatrist snapped, so I described what Peter looked like and all the details he had told me about his death, including the teddy bear. The psychiatrist was very taken aback but asked me some questions to pass on to Peter and soon I was passing information between them quite naturally.

Finally, the doctor said to my parents: 'There's nothing wrong with this girl. She's got ESP.'

I had no idea what he meant and asked if it was catching, which made the adults laugh.

'You've got a special gift,' the psychiatrist told me. 'You can talk to people who are dead. But you mustn't tell anyone because other people don't have it.'

I was only ten at this time, but as I entered my teens I realised his advice was good. If anybody found out I could talk to spirits, they would nag me the whole time, wanting me to contact their dead grandmothers or beloved pets or whatever. I just wanted to be a normal teenager, accepted for who I was and not labelled as 'weird' or 'different'. I was interested in fashion and boys – although being at a girls-only school I had little access to the opposite sex.

When I left school, I went to college to study fashion design and started making my own clothes. It was the early 1960s, and fashion college was an exciting place to be. One day I was crossing the road, wearing a white swing coat with two big black buttons that I had designed myself, when a car drove up and bumped into me, nudging my leg.

I leapt back and yelled, 'You idiot! What are you trying to do?' I recognised the driver as a young man I had seen in a jazz club but had never been introduced to.

'I'm trying to get to know you,' he said, grinning.

'Well, that's not the way to do it,' I snapped and stormed off.

A few weeks later I was in a coffee bar with some friends when the same guy walked in. Before I could say anything, one of my friends called out to him. 'Hey

Mike! Dorothy needs a lift home. You'll take her, won't you?'

The guy who had been supposed to take me hadn't turned up so I reluctantly accepted a lift from Mike, but as we drove home I made sure he knew that I had another boyfriend with whom I was due to go out that evening. I introduced him to my parents and left them chatting as I got changed and rushed out for the evening with my boyfriend. Imagine my surprise when I got home in time for my ten o'clock curfew to find Mike still there, still talking to Mum and Dad, obviously getting on with them like a house on fire.

I stopped, listened to my feelings, and realised that despite the way we had first met, I liked and trusted this guy. Although at that stage in my life I had turned away from my connection with spirit, I always had strong instincts about whether people were good or not, and he definitely was. Six months later we were married, and we had our son Carl in 1963, then our daughters, Nicky in '64 and Tanya in '66.

As a young mother I was kept very busy, working as a freelance dress designer as well as running our household. I'd told Mike about my psychic abilities, but the world of spirit wasn't something I had much time to think about. Then in 1972, my mother was taken ill with a severe cold and rushed to hospital. I drove up to visit her. She asked me to come close to her and she whispered, 'I don't think I'm going to make it this time.' I couldn't bear to hear it and said, 'No, Mum, you're wrong, you will make it.' The next morning I was getting ready for work when a voice in my head told me that she was going to die the next day. It even told me the time – eleven o'clock.

In my shock, I dismissed it. 'Go away,' I thought. 'I don't want to hear this. It can't be true.'

I had to work that day but I rang the hospital first thing and they told me Mum was absolutely fine – quite perky, in fact. And then at quarter past eleven I got the dreaded call to say that she had died very suddenly. I was filled with fierce anger. How could someone so good be taken? Having been warned in advance didn't help at all. In fact, I was angry with the spirits who had warned me and I pushed them all away in my grief.

I should have known that Mum would come back to me in spirit. Of course she would. The following year, when we were staying with my parents-in-law, I woke up in the night with an unbearably sharp pain in my chest, finding it extremely difficult to breathe. I'd never experienced anything like it in my life and was con-vinced I was dying but there was Mum's voice in my head, saying softly, 'Don't worry. You'll be OK.' I was rushed to hospital where they found I'd had a pulmonary embolism – a blood clot in the lungs. The doctors told Mike it would be touch and go whether I made it through the next twenty-four hours.

Meanwhile, my daughter Nicky, who was nine by this time, woke in the night and heard my mother's voice telling her that she wasn't to worry, that I'd been taken ill but that all would be well. The next morning when the news was broken over breakfast that I had been rushed to hospital and was very poorly, Nicky piped up: 'It's all right. Nana told me she will be fine.'

Of course, I recovered, and when I heard what Nicky had said, I realised that she has the same psychic abilities that I have. She gets visitors too.

Mike and I set up our own catering business that became very successful over the next few years but still I resisted listening to the voices in my head so we made mistakes. In particular, we changed the way our company was managed, even though I knew in my heart of hearts that it wasn't the right thing to do, and we ended up losing our business, with huge debts to pay off. We had to sell our house, all the antiques and pictures we had collected over the years, and even our youngest daughter Tanya's horse. It was a difficult time for all the family, and one of the lowest points in my life. It took us a long time to get back on our feet financially and decide what to do next.

A few years later, still searching, we moved in with my mother-in-law in Shaldon, South Devon, where we stayed for several months in a tiny room, cramped in with all our remaining possessions.

I went out for a walk along the cliffs one day, for some reason leaving my dog behind. I was lost in thought, just putting one foot in front of the other, when suddenly I looked down and realised that my toes were protruding right over the edge of the grass. The rocks on the beach were about a hundred feet below and I was more or less suspended over thin air. I'm not the kind of person who would ever consider suicide but I remember thinking, 'Oh well, I suppose it won't hurt for long.'

No sooner had I thought that than I felt my elbows being gripped firmly from behind and I was lifted off the ground, through the air and put down again behind a barbed wire fence a couple of yards further back. It was almost like being Mary Poppins. I sat down hard on the grass to get my breath back. What on earth had just happened? Who or what had saved my life?

The barbed wire was there to stop people getting too close to the unstable cliff edge and I'm not sure how I had managed to get on the wrong side of it, because my clothes weren't ripped at all. I was suddenly aware there was a hand beside me pointing across to the piece of turf I had been standing on. I then noticed that the turf was curved downwards because it was only three or four inches thick and the cliff was eroded away underneath. I should have fallen to my death.

I sat on that grass for a long time thinking about the feeling of those hands that had gripped my elbows and I realised I had been saved by two angels, one on either side. It wasn't my time to die. There was more I was supposed to do in this life and it was up to me to find it, but to do that I would have to open my mind to the areas I had been trying to ignore for so long. I had to start listening to the messages I received from angels and understanding that most things happen for a reason. It wasn't just by chance that I met Mike the day he nearly knocked me down – we were meant to be together. It wasn't by chance that we lost the catering business – I was supposed to do something else with my life.

Shortly after this, I was in a doctor's reception making an appointment when I heard the receptionist chatting to some nurses about someone who did tarot card readings. I asked who it was and was told there was a lady in Newton Abbot, not far from there.

'Are you interested?' a nurse asked.

I surprised myself by answering, 'Actually, I'm a medium myself.'

I went to see the woman in Newton Abbot and she looked up as I walked in. 'I've been waiting for you for five years,' she said. 'I knew you would come. There's a gold star over your head.'

More and more, the angels were nudging me to work with them but I was still held back by the fear that people would think I was stupid or weird, as they had when I was a child.

'Trust in us,' the voices in my head were saying. 'Have faith.'

The tarot woman told me that I was definitely going to become a professional psychic. I did a reading for her and she must have been impressed with what I told her because she began to recommend me to her friends, and it all took off without any form of advertising at all except word of mouth. It was as natural to me as breathing. Someone came in and sat opposite me, and voices would come into my head. I just had to pass on the words.

It was gratifying work, because I knew I was bringing comfort to a lot of people. When helping clients to get on with their lives after a bereavement, I could show them that the bond of love that had been there on earth was never lost. It felt like a worthwhile thing to be doing. Other people came with financial worries or business decisions to make, or emotional problems in a relationship, or fears for their children, and in all cases I tried to help them through the difficult times they faced.

One day a woman for whom I had done a reading came to me and said, 'I would love to learn how to do what you do. Would you teach me?'

I told her I didn't think I had anything to teach, but she thought otherwise. I had no teaching experience but when I considered it further I realised I could probably do it.

I spoke to a few other people and quickly put together a group of six students, which seemed like a good number. I had no idea what I was going to teach, so the night before I sat in my bath and talked to spirit and they gave me the whole format for the course, just like that. The next morning I stood up without any notes, trusting in spirit, and the words came out easily. I think my students were pleased with what they learned because at the end of the day, they all asked if they could come back for more. And then news of my course spread rapidly by word of mouth until I was travelling the world, teaching courses in loads of different countries to groups of ten people each time. It all happened generically without any planning. Someone would phone with an invitation and I'd agree to go and then more work would flow in as a result.

My own troubles weren't over, though. When my daughter Tanya was seven she was abused by someone in a position of trust and became very disturbed as a result.

I tried to pursue this man through the courts but was told it was his word against hers. All he got was a rap on the knuckles. It was a very hard time and I was deeply depressed about it all, yet trying to be calm and comfort my daughter as best I could.

One day I was taking a course in Guildford, Surrey, sixty miles away from where we were living at the time. I was walking up the high street towards the place where the course was due to take place when a little man wearing a dark brown raincoat came up and tapped me on the arm.

'Your mum wants to talk to you,' he said.

'No, she doesn't,' I said crossly.

'Yes, she does,' he insisted.

'My mother's dead!' I told him.

'I know *that*,' he said and I looked at him more closely. There was something very calm and still about him. 'I'm going where you're going,' he continued.

'How do you know where I'm going?'

In response, he walked ahead of me and turned into an alley then round to the back of the building where I was taking my course and in through the correct door. I was amazed as I followed him in, and finally ready to listen to what he had to say.

'Your mother is telling me that you feel as though you're facing a brick wall. But she says to remember that as each door closes a window opens, and don't you forget it.'

This was a phrase my mother had often used. I opened my mouth to thank him for the message but as quickly as he had arrived, he was gone again. Some people who were there for the course came over to greet me.

'Do you know that man?' I asked, pointing in the direction he had gone, but they all looked at each other blankly. No one did.

I never saw him again, but I believe he was a physical angel sent to bring me comfort at that very difficult time. Looking back, there was a kind of light about him and I trusted him instinctively. Reminding me of my mother's words about all the opportunities in the world was the perfect message for me at that time and knowing she was around helped me to pick myself – and my daughter – up again.

Most people think of angels as being in the spirit world, but I have learned that there are many different kinds. They have all ascended through many lifetimes and evolved in each so that their souls are pure. They communicate with us in different ways, but always for a reason, and listening to them will help us to move forwards in our lives.

Many wise angels have come to help me in different periods of my life. There were the five souls looking at me with love as I lay in my cot; the man in the brown suit who I thought was God; the two pairs of hands that lifted me back from the cliff edge in Devon; that little man in the main street in Guilford; and many, many more (I'll tell you about some of the others later in this book). I probably failed to recognise many angel visitations during the period between my teens and my thirties when I tried to turn my back on my psychic abilities. As I teach on my courses, the first thing you need to do is learn to be still and listen so that your sensitivity develops – and for a long time I wasn't listening.

Angels visit all of us at different times. By learning to recognise them and heed what they have to say, we can lead happier, more successful lives and find comfort to get us through the dark times. They may even save our lives.

Chapter 2

The Angels We Know

Once established, the bond of love is never broken. When someone who loves you passes away, they are not physically present on earth any more but they remain with you, watching over you, and they can help you when you need it. My mother only comes back to give me a message in periods when I have real problems but I know she's around the rest of the time and I still talk to her in my head every day.

Death isn't painful or difficult, even though dying can be. People fear letting go, but once you die you are going home, back to a place you recognise, somewhere you existed before your previous life on earth. Once you have arrived there, you turn around and see the pain your family is going through, and that's why many spirits come back as quickly as they can to try and give comfort. If someone comes to me for a reading soon after a bereavement, the spirit will often just say, 'Tell them I love them and that I'm fine.'

I was in a supermarket recently, squeezing some lemons to see if they were juicy, and I got into conversation with a woman there. Suddenly her husband's voice came into my head, saying, 'Tell Margaret that she did everything she possibly could and that she's to stop feeling guilty. Nothing more could have been done.'

I turned to the woman. 'Are you Margaret?' I asked.

'Yes.' She looked puzzled that I should know her name.

I repeated the message from her husband and she was visibly shocked.

'Oh my goodness,' she said. 'Oh my goodness. He died last week and I've been feeling so guilty because I went out shopping and when I got back he was dead. He'd been ill with multiple sclerosis for a long time and I'd been nursing him, but I didn't realise the end was so near and I went out to get some food.' She began to sob and we hugged each other for several minutes until she calmed down.

'He's with you all the time,' I told her. 'He wants you to be happy.'

People always come back for their own funerals – not to see how many friends turn up, or whether their funeral instructions have been followed, because these are earthly concerns that no longer matter. Instead they come to give comfort to those they have left behind, in whatever way they can. Without exception, I have seen the dead person at every funeral I have ever gone to. Every one. And at my father's funeral, he actually sat on his own coffin smoking and drinking throughout!

My dad had been a military man, so his coffin was draped in a Union Jack and there were just a few poppies on it – the wreaths were all outside the church. I had agreed with my brother and sister that I would say a few words during the service but as the time drew near, I wasn't sure I could do it. My father had been ninety years old, which is a good age, but I'd always been a daddy's girl and I was very, very upset about his death. I wasn't sure I would be able to make my little speech without breaking down because I was feeling so over-whelmed, but when the time came, I looked up and there was Dad, sitting on his coffin with his legs crossed – and he winked at me. He had a cigarette in one hand, a beer in the other and he looked cheerful and calm, and that gave me the courage to go on. I stood up and started talking about all the good deeds he had done in his life, and the sort of person he was, and in my head I could hear him say, 'Go on, that's my girl!'

Not everyone is able to see spirits at a funeral but many people have described to me a sudden feeling that the dead person is close to them, or hugging them, or has an arm round their shoulder. Maybe they can smell their perfume or hear a familiar voice inside their head, and at that point they get a sense of strength and know that they will be able to cope with whatever happens next.

Family members on the other side will not watch and listen to every single thing we do, but they always know when we are thinking about them. Some will become our guardian angels, who can come to help us when we are straying off our life's path and to give us comfort and guidance at different stages when we need it. There are many different ways they can communicate with us – and one of the most common is actually hearing their voice in our head.

Lock the Doors!

Anne was a woman in her mid-40s who ran her own little florist's business. She loved the work, because it allowed her to express her creativity and she got to spend her days surrounded by the beautiful colours and scents of flowers, but most weeks she only just scraped by and sometimes she had trouble finding the rent. Here's a story she told me about her visit from an angel.

It was the day before Mother's Day and I had done a roaring trade for a change, as dozens of customers ordered hand-tied bouquets to be delivered to their mums. At six o'clock, I closed the shop, put all the takings into a canvas bag and walked out to my car to take the money to the bank. They had a late-night deposit slot where I could put it in, ready to be counted the next day. I threw the canvas bag onto the floor on the passenger side of the car, where it was clearly visible, and set off through the rush-hour traffic.

I was just coming up to a set of traffic lights when I felt my skin pricking all over and heard my mother's voice in my head. 'Lock the doors! Lock the doors!' it said.

Without thinking, I pressed the central locking knob and there was a click. Seconds later a motorcyclist in a blue helmet with a black visor yanked at the handle of the passenger door and rattled it angrily. When it wouldn't open, he pounded on the window so hard I was sure he was going to break the glass. Fortunately the lights changed at that point and I put my foot down and drove off as fast as I could to the bank, looking anxiously in the mirror in case I was being followed. When I got to the deposit slot, I drove round several times to make sure the motorcyclist hadn't come after me before I dared to get out of the car.

I was very shaken. If the takings from the shop had been stolen by that motorcyclist my business would probably have gone bust. I needed the Mother's Day income to make up for lean periods in the rest of the year. I'm convinced it was my mother's voice that had made me lock the door, but it was two years since my mum had died so how was that possible?

Anne came to see me for a reading and I explained to her that the incident had happened so that she could learn that her mother is still taking care of her. She said she couldn't believe that the voice was quite so clear, almost as though her mum was sitting in the passenger seat of the car. She told me that from now on she is always going to lock the car doors when she drives her takings to the bank.

Of course, not all bad things can be prevented. The reason that theft was prevented is because it wasn't part of Anne's life plan for her business to go bust. I still see her now and her business is ticking over – not making a fortune but bringing a lot of happiness to her and to all the people who receive her beautiful creations as gifts.

If you hear a loved one's voice in your head, you may question whether it is real or just your imagination, and sometimes it can be hard to distinguish, but the key question to ask is whether you were thinking about that person, or something to do with them, at the time. If you weren't, and the voice just came out of nowhere, it is likely to be a message from the spirit world.

Trekking in the Blue Mountains

We all have a time at which we are ordained to die, according to a blueprint that was set down before we came into this life. So, for example, one person might be ordained to die of cancer at the age of eighty-three while another might be supposed to go in a car accident at the age of twenty.

It's a strange concept to get your head around that the time of your death is pre-ordained. All of us have lived many different lifetimes and with each one, we have to learn specific lessons in order for our souls to evolve. You will come back into a circumstance that enables you to learn the specific lesson you need to learn next, and your life will be as long as it needs to be for that purpose. Maybe you need to learn compassion for others, or not to place such a high value on material possessions, or how to express your creativity. There are all sorts of lessons to learn.

Guardian angels might intervene if you are straying away from your purpose, or having difficulty overcoming a problem that you need to overcome – or if your life is about to be cut short unexpectedly. Their warnings can help us to avoid dying early – if we only listen to them.

A man I knew received a warning while trekking in Australia's Blue Mountains, just north of Sydney.

Two friends and I set off on a bush walk well armed with information from the tourist authority about the route we were taking and hazards to avoid on the way. There was even a little leaflet with pictures of dangerous creatures, such as snakes and spiders, we might encounter, but we were reassured by the advice that snakes will do their best to avoid contact with humans. If they hear footsteps approaching, they will slither off down a hole or into the nearest brush. For this reason, you are advised to make as much noise as you can when walking into an overgrown area.

The sandstone mountains have a blueish tinge when viewed from a distance and the walk we were on was quite spectacular. It was a clear, sunny day and we covered about twenty miles before we decided to stop and set up camp for the night in a flattish, sheltered area. We collected some firewood and built a fire then balanced a pot of water on top to make tea. We had brought bread and cheese, cold meat and fruit, but as the light began to fade, the air grew cooler and I was glad of the fire.

We sat drinking our tea, eating our food and chatting about our day. I was about to stand up to walk off behind a tree and relieve myself when I heard my dad's voice in my head, clear as a bell, saying, 'Be still!'

I froze, shocked to hear him, because my father had died of cancer the previous year. We'd been very close and, in fact, he'd been the one who introduced me to the joys of trekking in the bush.

At that moment my eye was caught by a slight movement in the grass just inches from my outstretched leg. A brown snake was slithering towards me, so well camouflaged by the dry vegetation that I hadn't noticed it till that moment. It was too late to jump up and run away because it was within striking distance.

My heart was pounding as I tried to remember the pictures in that tourist leaflet. Was a plain brown snake poisonous? I could feel beads of sweat springing out on my face. My friends were facing in the opposite direction, watching the sunset on the hills and oblivious to my situation. I didn't dare shout to them, didn't dare breathe, as the snake lifted its head and started to slither over my bare leg. I suppose it thought it was a log.

My father's words – 'Be still!' – echoed in my head and I felt amazingly calm, feeling the cool roughness of the snake's skin against my own.

It was about a metre long, and had probably crossed my leg within thirty seconds but those seconds felt much longer than normal seconds, as though time was suspended. Once past, the snake headed off into the undergrowth without a backward glance.

As soon as I was sure it was well out of the way, I reached into my rucksack to look for the tourist authority leaflet on snakes, and straight away I saw a picture looking exactly like the creature I had just encountered. The text underneath read: 'The Eastern Brown Snake is the second most venomous snake in the world. They are reluctant to bite but if they do, their venom is highly toxic and can be fatal within two hours. They react to movement so if you come close to one, stay completely still and it will ignore you.'

My father's advice to be still had possibly saved my life. My mouth was so dry and my throat so tight that it was some time before I could speak to tell my friends what had just happened. But I felt a warm comfort in the knowledge that my dad was still protecting me just as he used to in the past when I was a kid. It was a very spiritual experience.

Missing the Ferry

Sometimes it takes an intervention from more than one guardian angel before the message gets across. A woman called Marjorie told me a story about a narrow escape she and her family experienced while on holiday in March 1987.

My husband and I had taken our two children, aged eight and ten, on a camping holiday in the Netherlands. We'd toured around, stopping at different campsites, and had a lovely time exploring the countryside. On the day we were booked to catch the ferry home, we started to drive towards the port, but I heard a voice in my head saying, 'There's plenty of time. No need to rush.' It sounded like my dead mother's voice but I'd never had a psychic experience before so I didn't think anything of it.

'We're very early,' I said to my husband, 'And there will be nothing to do at the ferry terminal.' We were passing a town that looked very pretty. 'Why don't we stop here, have a look around and a bite to eat and we can get going in an hour's time?'

He agreed that it would be daft to rush all the way there and have to sit in a concrete ferry terminal for ages, so we parked the car and strolled along the pretty streets of the town, looking in shop windows and admiring the spring flowers in the gardens. We sat down in a café and ordered some food, but the café suddenly got busy and the waiters were very slow bringing our order. My husband was glancing at his watch and beginning to feel stressed by the time we'd finished eating and paid the bill.

We left the café and walked back towards our car, but as we rounded the corner we saw a crowd of people gathered around it. What on earth had happened? As we got closer, we saw that an elderly man was lying on the road just by our car, with a badly broken leg. I could actually see the bone sticking out at an angle and it made me feel sick to look at it. He was moaning quietly as someone tucked a folded-up jacket under his head to act as a pillow. I couldn't understand what the bystanders were saying and wasn't sure whether he had been knocked over or had just fallen badly, but there was no way we could move our car. We would have to wait until the ambulance arrived and the man was taken away.

Within a few minutes an ambulance pulled up with lights flashing, but the ambulance staff took a long time examining the elderly man where he lay on the ground. They put an oxygen mask on him, listened to his chest and tied splints to his leg. We didn't have mobile phones back then but my husband went into a public phone box nearby to try to ring the ferry port and tell them we were running late. He speaks a smattering of German and hoped he would be able to make them understand, but he couldn't get through to anyone who seemed to have a clue what he was saying.

At last, the elderly man was lifted into the ambulance and we were able to jump in our car and get on our way, but by this time we had only forty minutes left to get to the port – Zeebrugge – and we were about an hour's drive away. My husband put his foot down and did his best to get us there but as we turned the corner into the ferry terminal, we were just in time to see it chugging away.

'It's only just gone!' I moaned. 'Look – they haven't even closed the back door yet.'

Dejected, we turned back to the ferry office where we found someone who spoke English but he explained that all the ferries for the rest of the day were fully booked and we wouldn't be able to get another one until early the next morning. By this stage we were running very short of money but we didn't know of any campsites in the vicinity so we drove to the outskirts of Zeebrugge where we found a reasonably cheap hotel in a back street and booked in there for our last night.

We all felt a bit flat as we tried to fill the remaining hours of our holiday. I remember hearing lots of police cars and ambulance sirens and wondered if there was some kind of drill going on. A woman was crying in the foyer of our hotel but I didn't speak the language so couldn't attempt to ask her what was wrong.

We had an early night and as we set off for the port the next morning I remember seeing a picture of a ferry on the front covers of some newspapers in a newsstand. Still, I thought nothing of it until we arrived at the terminal and found that it was blocked off with police cordons. We got out to ask what was going on.

'Have you not heard?' an official told us. 'The *Herald of Free Enterprise* sank yesterday as it left the port.'

'But we were supposed to be on it!' I exclaimed, and I felt the blood draining from my face.

'You and ten others missed it,' he told me.

I was deeply shocked when I heard the whole story. One hundred and ninety-three people died on that ferry and if we had caught it, it could have been one hundred and ninety-seven. Those back doors that I'd noticed were still open as the ferry sailed off had caused it to let in water and sink not long after it left the port. I remembered my mother's voice in my head and knew that it had been her who saved us that day. I've got no doubt about it at all. The suggestion that we should 'take our time' just came into my head, in her voice, and it saved my family from drowning in a horrible tragedy. I still feel very shaken whenever I think about it, and overwhelmed with gratitude for the help we received.

I believe that several angels were at work that day to save Marjorie's family. There was her mother, of course, but there were also the angels who made the café they chose suddenly get busy so as to slow them down, and then the old man's accident was caused by an angel in a way that also served a purpose in his life. Their time simply hadn't come and they were not supposed to be on that ferry.

The Red Striped Motorbike

It's not just mothers and fathers who can come back with warnings. Any relative you were close to can come with a message; I have even heard of great-grandparents who had never actually met the person in question bringing advice, but in those instances they tended to be a well-known family character who everyone was familiar with.

One woman I know got a message from her grandmother and was asked to pass it on to her son. Maybe he wasn't listening and that's why his mother had to be the go-between, but this is how it happened.

Sarah had a very disturbing dream one night. She saw a boy's severed head rolling along the ground in a motorcycle helmet, and she saw the bike lying on its side with red stripes on the bodywork. Her grandmother's voice came through in the dream, saying, 'Please don't get it. Please don't.'

The very next afternoon her twenty-year-old son Nicolas popped in for tea, looking very pleased with himself.

'I've just put down a deposit on a motorbike,' he said. 'I've been wanting one for ages and this is perfect, and at the right price too.'

Sarah froze in her tracks. 'It doesn't by any chance have red stripes down the sides, does it?'

He stared at her in astonishment. 'How on earth did you know that?'

She told him about her dream and begged him not to buy the bike. Now, most boys his age wouldn't listen to their mother going on about a dream they'd had, but Nicolas was a very sensitive boy, and something about her dream struck a chord. He'd been having some dreams himself – vague ones he couldn't remember well when he woke up in the morning, but he sensed there had been a warning in them.

'I can't really afford to lose the deposit,' he said, 'but I'll see what I can do.'

'Don't worry,' Sarah said. 'I'll pay you back the money so long as you promise me you won't buy the bike.'

She didn't have to do that, though, because Nicolas asked around amongst his friends to see if anyone else was interested in buying that particular bike. Sure enough, his friend Greg said he'd be delighted – it was exactly the kind of bike he'd been looking for.

And then a month after he took delivery of the bike, Greg was killed in an accident caused by mechanical failure of a crucial part of the bike.

Nicolas was devastated and blamed himself for a while, and his mother came to see me to talk about it all. I explained to her that it had been Greg's time to die but it hadn't been Nicolas's and so there was no point in blame. Even though none of us would want someone we know to come to harm, it's the law of the universe that there is a time to leave our body, and circumstances will arise at that time in order to help our soul on its journey.

What Nicolas has to do now is work out why his life was saved. There must be some purpose, some mission that he has to fulfil, and he should concentrate on finding that and living the rest of his life well. Sarah told me that he has started talking to his great-grandmother and asking her advice, which is a fantastic idea. I'm sure he'll go on to live a very valuable life now.

Dodgy Electrics

It doesn't need to be a blood relative who becomes your guardian angel. Children who were adopted with love may be looked after by their adoptive parent after death. Even if you fell out in later life, the love your parents or relatives had for you as a baby is the important thing. Brothers and sisters, close friends and partners can also become your guardian angel after their death and they will remain so for as long as you need them. The people who care for you in the spirit world will never move on to another life as long as you are still on earth and possibly needing their support. That is their choice, not yours.

After a bereavement, I have often heard of people being told that they have to 'let go' and 'move on', but this is wrong, because it's not them holding on. The person who has passed over decides to be with us, in order to help us in our time of need, and they will choose when it is the right time to move on.

There's a man called Kurt, an actor based in New York and LA, who always comes to me for readings whenever I'm in either of those cities. He told me the following story:

I was in my trailer one morning just waiting to be called on set. I was feeling nervous because it was the first day of filming and no matter how many movies you've done, the first day is always nerve-racking. What's more, I had agreed to do a couple of my own stunts in this movie, and that morning I had to jump from one building to another attached to a safety wire. My makeup had been done, and I didn't have many lines to remember, but I kept going over the sequence of the action in my head, trying to make it second nature so that the director could capture the scene in as few takes as possible.

All of a sudden, I heard my brother's voice in my head – a child's voice. He had died of meningitis when he was six years old and I was only four but I had very clear memories of him. That morning in the unit I hadn't been thinking about him at all, but suddenly there he was in my head, and he was saying the words 'Electrics' and 'Careful'. I got the spookiest feeling and my skin felt sensitised, as if something was brushing against it. Somehow I just knew I had to take this seriously.

I found the assistant director and asked him if he could please check all the electrics for me.

'It's all checked,' he said cheerfully. 'It's OK. It's fine.'

'I don't want to be a pain in the ass,' I said, 'but please could you check again? I just have a strong feeling something is wrong with the electrics.'

I didn't tell them about my brother because I didn't want to get a reputation as a complete lunatic. As it was, I was taking a risk by making them recheck everything because time is money on a film set and there are always other actors out there who are hungry for your job. The assistant director called over the stunt co-ordinator and he agreed that he would have another look through everything for me.

'Oh my God!' Suddenly a shout went up from the top of the building I was supposed to be jumping off.

'What is it?' The stunt co-ordinator ran up to find out, with me following close behind.

'A lamp has fallen over onto the safety wire. It can't have been sandbagged properly.' Everyone looked at each other, ashen-faced, then turned to me.

'What would have happened if it hadn't been spotted?' I asked, trying to keep my voice from shaking.

'The safety wire wouldn't have worked when you jumped, and on top of that you ran a risk of being electrocuted.'

I would have died, in other words.

Kurt came to ask me to explain to him how his brother, who died at the age of six, could have known about safety trip wires. I told him that once he died, his brother was not a child any more but a pure soul. He could see where things were going to go wrong and he saved Kurt, because he was meant to be saved at that point. Since then, his brother has been in contact with him several times during readings, and Kurt follows his advice on all kinds of matters. Well, you would after such a narrow escape, wouldn't you?

After an Accident

I heard from a friend about another incident when a child was the angel who came back to save a life. A taxi driver called Harry had lost his little girl to a rare childhood cancer when she was only seven years old. Three years later, Harry's taxi was in a multiple pile-up on a motorway.

I saw there had been an accident up ahead and I pushed my foot to the floor and just managed to stop before I hit the cars involved. But no sooner had I come to a standstill than there was a huge jolt as I was shunted from behind and forced into the front two cars, and then the world went black.

Suddenly a face appeared in the blackness, and when I focused I realised it was my daughter Jasmine. She looked beautiful, her blonde hair gleaming and a lovely smile on her face. She was talking to me but it took me a while to make out the words.

'Daddy, it's not your time to die. Call for help.'

I couldn't make sense of it at first so she repeated the words. It was then I remembered about the accident. Perhaps she was right. Perhaps I should call for help. But what I really wanted was to stay there with her.

'Call for help, Daddy,' she urged again, and this time I obeyed.

My voice sounded very weak and pathetic when I first tried, so I called again, and suddenly I heard voices breaking through the blackness.

'I think this one here's alive,' a voice said. 'I'm sure I heard him trying to speak.'

Then I heard another voice. 'There's a pulse. It's very weak but it's there. Can you hear me, sir?'

I wanted to say yes but I didn't have the strength. I stayed vaguely aware of what was going on as they used cutting equipment to free me from the wreck of my cab then transferred me onto a stretcher and took me to hospital. I didn't want to regain full consciousness because while I remained in my semi-conscious state I could feel my daughter was still there, comforting me.

When I came round fully, I was told that the ambulancemen had originally written me off as dead. They wouldn't have tried to resuscitate me if they hadn't heard a faint noise coming from my lips. My daughter Jasmine saved my life that day by urging me to call out.

I spoke to Harry on the phone after I heard this story and explained to him that Jasmine is with him all the time, not just when he's in danger. She's beside him when he's driving his cab, at home watching TV and even when he's asleep. Just because he can't see her doesn't mean she's not there, and he can speak to her any time he likes. Then, when it is his time to die, she will be there waiting for him, ready to take him over to the other side.

It Wasn't Her Time

Nurses deal with death all the time and they tend to be very sensitive to the whole process. When they walk onto the ward in the morning, they can often sense which patients are going to die that day. If they're not too busy, they can judge when to call the relatives to come and say goodbye, and, if there's no time for that, they will sit with a dying patient themselves, holding their hand as they take their last breaths and slip peacefully away. Most nurses tend to be spiritual people with heightened awareness that helps them to notice messages from the other side. Here's one nurse's story of an angel intervention that really affected her.

I'd settled all the patients down for the night and was about to go and have a coffee in the nurses' station when I saw a man standing in the ward. I turned to go and have a word with him but when I got there I couldn't see him any more. The light was dim so I thought nothing more of it and went for my coffee.

Half an hour later, I saw the same man standing by the bed of one of my patients, down at the end of the ward. I walked along there and as I got closer I realised that he must be a spirit because his features were fuzzy and there was a kind of glow around him. His face looked beautiful as he gazed down at the elderly woman in the bed.

'Is she your wife?' I asked him.

'She is my beloved,' he replied, and I was struck by the old-fashioned phrase.

I looked at the lady in the bed and realised she was barely breathing. I pressed the call button and a colleague came hurrying up and together we worked hard to resuscitate her. By the time the doctor on call got there, she had a regular heartbeat again and he said that we had almost certainly saved her life.

When I discussed it with my colleague later, we agreed that the woman's 'beloved' had made himself visible so that we would react. He had saved her life, not us. I found it very comforting because I had lost my mother at the age of fourteen and I've always had a feeling that she protects me but this was the proof I needed.

If you have a feeling that a loved one is protecting you and acting as your guardian angel, then it is true. Which relatives or friends do you believe are watching over you in spirit? I expect you have a very clear idea because they will have let you know by giving you a 'feeling' about it. These 'feelings' are your loved one's way of letting you know that they're there. Just as they can put words into your head, so they can put 'feelings' and emotions. As we will discuss next, they can even put an arm round your shoulder.

Delivering a Warning

Most people report hearing their friend's or relative's voice during a visitation, but some 'feel' their presence as well. It's a sense memory, similar to the feeling you had when you were in the womb. You can feel a feather-light touch on your face, the weight of a hand on your shoulder, or maybe just a tightening of your skin all over. Many people have described feeling an arm around their shoulders at times of trouble, and then experiencing an overwhelming sense that things will be all right. If it is an angel they knew on earth, whether that person died a week before, or thirty or forty years before, they get a sense inside their head of who it is. You don't necessarily hear the voice; sometimes there is just what I call an 'inner knowing'.

Pure souls are omnipresent. The physical body doesn't weigh them down any more so they can be with you at your work, with your sister in her car, and with your child at school, looking after every single family member at the same time.

Our guardian angels can come to bring comfort or they can come with a warning. Sometimes the message is as clear as crystal and other times it is just a general piece of advice to take care, as in this story about a woman called Donna.

I was standing at the sink doing the washing-up, not thinking about anything in particular, when suddenly I felt my mother was there and I picked up a clean tea-towel to hand to her so she could start drying. Then I stopped. What was I doing? My mother had died fifteen years before.

My brain had often played tricks on me in the past (or so I thought). I'd be in the middle of some chore when the thought would come into my head: 'Call your mother. You haven't spoken to her for a while.' And I'd think, 'Oh, I must do it,' before remembering that she is dead and I can't call her any more.

But that day in the kitchen, the feeling that she was present was so strong that I just knew something was wrong. I dropped the tea-towel and called my husband at work.

'Are you OK?' I asked.

'Yeah, fine,' he said. 'Why wouldn't I be?'

I rang the school to check if our son was OK, and they said he was fine but I still had a funny feeling that we had to be extra-cautious.

The next morning, a Saturday, the three of us were going shopping together and we were in a hurry to get going, but I was still aware of this strange sense of unease. I was just reversing out of the driveway when all of a sudden my husband yelled 'Stop!' so I slammed my foot hard on the brake.

At that point a lorry came thundering round the corner at top speed and clipped the back of our car. The crunching noise was horrible but we were all unharmed. It was only when I got out to look at the damage, I realised that if I hadn't braked when I did, that lorry would have gone straight into the back seat of the car where our son was sitting. And then I looked at the passenger seat where my husband had been and realised there was no way he could actually have seen the lorry coming from that angle.

'Why did you shout "Stop"?' I asked him.

'I've got absolutely no idea,' he said. 'I didn't consciously think anything. The words just came out of my mouth.'

I realised then that my mother had come back to warn me to be careful and her intervention had probably saved our son's life. Since then, whenever I get a thought in my head that I should call her, I make sure I sit down somewhere quiet and have a little conversation with her in my mind. She's looking out for me, and at last I have learned to listen.

I believe that Donna's mother not only put the thought into her head that she should be cautious, but she also put the word 'Stop!' into her husband's mouth. She wasn't taking any chances with the safety of her beloved family.

Father Knows Best

In this instance a woman called Margaret, who lives in Cumbria, was saved from a horrible accident by her father.

It was a bitterly cold day in March and I was walking my two young sons to school. We were wrapped up warmly but still the driving sleet stung our faces. We stopped at a newsagent's and I picked up a newspaper while the boys got a packet of crisps each. It was a relief to reach the warmth of the school, but then I faced the prospect of the journey home again. I decided to catch a bus back but I waited and waited at the stop without any sign of one so eventually I realised I would have to walk again.

There were some tiny lambs in the field opposite the newsagent's so I thought I would go and have a look, worried about how they were coping with the freezing weather. I was about to step off the pavement when I heard my father's voice just by my right ear: 'Go and buy a paper.' Dad had died twelve years earlier. I shook my head. It was silly. I already had a paper that I'd bought earlier. Disregarding the voice, I stepped into the road to cross over.

The voice was angry now. 'Do as you're bloody well told. Go and buy a paper!'

I'd never argued with my father when he was alive and I wasn't about to start now he was dead, so I turned and went back to the newsagent's. I'd just bent down to pick up a *Daily Mail* when there was a screech of brakes outside and then an almighty clattering sound.

The newsagent and I rushed out to find that a lorry had skidded and a huge pile of girders strapped on the back had come loose and fallen off onto the pavement at exactly the spot where I had been planning to stand and watch the lambs. I was so shaken, I sat down on the kerb, sleet or no sleet. Dad had saved my life.

Once my heart had stopped racing, I went back inside to pay for my *Daily Mail*. When I got home and opened it, between the pages there was a white feather and I felt instinctively that was a sign from Dad telling me he'd been there.

Finding a tiny white feather after an angel visitation is quite common. It's like a little calling card from the other side. I'll explain more about this on page 98.

The Smell of Smoke

Some people report smelling a scent similar to one worn by their relative, such as the lavender eau de parfum of a favourite granny, or a flower that your mother was especially fond of. A lady called Jane told me the following story about the way her father let her know he was still around:

I had just split up with my husband and moved into a place of my own, so it was a very difficult time. One Sunday afternoon I was tidying up when all of a sudden I smelled a familiar smell of cigar smoke. It was exactly the same as the cigar my father used to smoke after lunch on a Sunday – but he had been dead for three years.

I sat down and sniffed, and the smell just got stronger and stronger. Suddenly I knew that Dad was there with me, in the room. I cried a little bit, and then I started talking to him, telling him what was happening in my life. I knew instinctively that I didn't need to talk out loud – I could tell him things in my head. It was a huge comfort to feel his presence and it really lifted my spirits.

As the smell began to fade, I said 'Dad, please keep coming back. Come as often as you can.'

From then on, I started to smell his cigar smoke every Sunday afternoon, around the same time, and I would sit down and have a chat with him in my head. It helped me a lot in that difficult period, and one day I mentioned it to a girlfriend of mine.

'Why don't I come over to your flat and see if I can smell it?' she asked, and I agreed.

The following Sunday she came, along with another friend. One of them said straight away, 'Oh my goodness, I can certainly smell it.'

The other looked doubtful. 'I think I can,' she said, screwing up her nose. Then, all of a sudden, she cried out. 'Oh my! I think he just blew a cloud of cigar smoke in my face!'

I knew that he was giving me absolute proof that he was there with me. I never smelled cigar smoke on any other day of the week, but every Sunday afternoon it was there. I asked him questions about anything I wanted to discuss and I could hear his answers in my head and in my heart.

I think it is very touching that her father chose to make his presence known in a period of Jane's life when she really needed support. He helped her to get through difficult times and start to enjoy life again.

An Angel Set Me Free

We expect our parents to die before us. It's the logical way of things, and it feels wrong, as if the universe has been turned upside down, if one of your children dies before you. Many clients have first come to me when they are struggling to understand why this can happen, and why it should have happened to them, and I am able to give them comfort by explaining what I know and contacting their lost child for them.

After such a shocking event as a child's death, it's human nature to look for someone or something to blame: a drunk driver, an over-tired doctor, faulty electrics, or whatever. But imagine what it is like if a child of yours takes their own life? Who do you have to blame? In Stella's case, she blamed herself.

Josh was twenty-three years old when he committed suicide by jumping off a tall building. I knew he was upset about breaking up with his girlfriend but I had absolutely no idea how distressed he was. Why didn't he come to me? Why didn't I know? As a mother, surely I should have realised instinctively that he needed help? I tortured myself with thoughts of what his last moments must have been like, and as the weeks and months passed I sank into a depression so deep that I didn't think I would ever recover. It was like being in a dark, enclosed prison cell. I couldn't bring myself to get up in the mornings and I don't think I would have carried on living myself if it hadn't been for my other son, Callum. I couldn't put him through another loss.

One day I was sitting on the edge of my bed in my pyjamas trying to will myself to get up. I hadn't had a shower or washed my hair for about two weeks. My clothes were all dirty. The room was dusty. Everything was falling apart. Suddenly I heard a voice.

'It's about time you got yourself a life.'

It sounded like Josh's voice but when I looked around the room I couldn't see anyone. 'Who said that? Is that you, Josh?'

''Course it's me, Mum.'

My heart leapt. 'Are you OK? Where are you?' There was no answer to my question but somehow I felt he was still there. I got up and made a cup of tea then I decided to have a shower. As I stood under the hot water, soaping my hair, I heard music playing. I stuck my head out and realised it was Josh's music, and it was coming from his room.

I got out of the shower, dried myself and wandered through, and somehow his CD player had been switched on and was playing one of his favourite CDs. But there was no one else in the house apart from me. I didn't feel scared, though. I knew it was Josh, and it made me smile.

Down in the kitchen, over lunch, I kept trying to talk to him again. 'I hope you're all right,' I said. 'Are you all right?'

I was just pouring a cup of coffee when I heard him say, 'I'm all right, Mum. You're the one who's not. I'm sorry I didn't say goodbye but I'm happy with the life I've got now. It's time you started living again. Don't waste the life you've got.'

The words were so clear that it was as if he was sitting across the kitchen table from me. Instantly I felt as though I'd been released from a prison of pain. The heaviness that had been weighing me down and preventing me from doing anything lifted. My head cleared. The room seemed brighter. I felt physically lighter.

That afternoon I did several loads of laundry and some housework. I phoned my older son and asked him round for dinner then I went to the local shops to buy some delicious food and cooked it. I felt like myself again.

For months I'd been trapped inside my own grief. It took my son coming back as an angel to set me free.

Stella came to see me and was able to communicate with Josh again, but it was that first time that made all the difference. She knew he was fine, and that was the main thing that helped her to move on.

Seeing Our Loved Ones Again

Actually seeing the guardian angels who come to bring advice or warnings is much less common than hearing them or sensing their presence. It uses a lot of energy for a spirit to take on human form and it's not usually necessary. Since my mother died, I've only seen her a couple of times.

On one occasion my daughter Tanya was very ill after suffering a huge allergic reaction to ibuprofen. Her heart actually failed, she was rushed in to hospital and I was told it was touch and go whether she would make it through the night. As I paced up and down in the patients' lounge, blaming myself, as parents do, wondering whether I could have done anything differently, suddenly I saw my mother's face in a little oval cameo. Her hair was very dark, as it was when she was younger, and she was wearing blue, her favourite colour, and I knew she had come to let me know things would be all right. Sure enough, Tanya survived the night and didn't suffer any ill effects from her experience, although she has to wear a warning bracelet at all times now.

A lady called June told me about her own experience of seeing her husband, who had died the year before.

Life was very, very tough for me. I had four young children, very little money, and my husband had just dropped dead from a heart attack at the age of only forty, without any life insurance. I was crawling through the days under a blanket of depression, just existing rather than living. And then one day I walked into the sitting room and there was my husband, sitting in his usual chair, with his legs crossed, smiling at me.

I think my knees gave way beneath me I was so shocked, and I sank down onto the sofa. I stared at him open-mouthed for a while. He obviously wasn't solid flesh and bone like a living human being, but he was clear enough, with a kind of glow about him.

'Richard?' I asked tentatively, tears coming to my eyes.

'It's time you got your act together,' he said, looking straight at me.

'What do you mean?'

'You need to start living again. I will do everything I can to help you.'

And then he disappeared, leaving me absolutely stunned. I had no doubt it was him, but I thought I would never be able to tell anyone or they'd lock me up in the loony bin or try to put me on happy pills. I kept thinking about what he had said, and wondering how he would be able to help me. My problems were very real and of this world.

A few weeks later, I had some bills to pay and no idea how I was going to pay them. I walked into the sitting room and suddenly heard my husband's voice saying, 'Green folder, top shelf.' I went straight up to the bedroom, looked in the green folder on the top shelf and found a building society book for an account I hadn't known about with easily enough money to cover the bills in it. That was a fantastic gift.

From then on, I kept hearing Richard's voice at the oddest times, often cracking little jokes. He'd always been able to make me laugh, and now he was making me laugh again after his death. He's a very witty man.

A friend of his, John, used to visit every week to see if I needed help with any odd jobs. He was a lovely person and we enjoyed talking about Richard together and reminding each other of things he had said and done. One day, four years after Richard had died, I heard his voice in my head saying, 'You should marry John.'

'I can't!' I cried out loud. 'I miss you too much.'

'It's time to move on,' he said.

Next time John came round, I looked at him with different eyes and realised that I could be attracted to him if I just let myself. I also got the feeling that he might possibly be attracted to me. To cut a long story short, a year later we were married, as Richard had suggested. He doesn't come to visit me so much any more now, but I know he is always there, looking out for me and for our children.

Black Ice

As I said before, our time of death is pre-ordained, but I believe there are actually two points at which we can die – an earlier and a later one. We each have two 'buttons to press': one of these gives us the longest possible time on earth and the other gives us the shortest.

It's wrong to believe that God 'takes' us. He gives us life in the first place and it's up to us what we do with it. If you are not learning the life lessons you are supposed to learn in this lifetime, you can go early and then you will have to reincarnate next time with the same lessons to learn. But before that your guardian angel may come to warn you and help you get on the right track.

In the following story, Lisa had a lesson to learn – and I'm glad to say that she listened.

I was driving along a narrow country road with my boyfriend one winter afternoon. Suddenly the car hit an invisible patch of black ice and hurtled into an uncontrollable spin. I felt as though I was floating in a bubble, as though time was in slow motion. I couldn't hear anything and I knew there was nothing I could do because it makes it worse if you brake during a skid. Suddenly I saw my father's face right in front of me, smiling. It was very clear and detailed, right down to his sparkly blue eyes.

Next there was an almighty crash and everything came to a standstill. I didn't feel a jolt, though, because it was as if there was a pillow cushioning me. Once we were stationary, I looked down. The windscreen had shattered and I had fragments of glass all over me, sparkling in the sunlight. There was a bit of broken wing mirror in my hair. I looked round at my boyfriend and he was covered in glass as well but seemed fine.

It was difficult getting out of the car because the doors were all bent and twisted, but someone came and helped us, telling us that we had smashed into his van. He seemed very shaken and kept giving us strange looks.

'You'd better get away in case it catches fire,' he said. 'I've called for an ambulance.'

I looked at my boyfriend. 'I don't think we need an ambulance,' I said. 'I feel fine.'

It was then I turned to look at the car and couldn't believe my eyes. It had been ripped almost in two, had lost two of its wheels, and the fuel tank had ruptured and was leaking petrol all over the road.

A police car arrived soon afterwards and, after inspecting the car, a policeman said to us: 'If I'd come on that without knowing any better, I'd have assumed someone had died in there and that I'd need a fire engine to cut out their body.'

When the ambulance pulled up, they treated the lorry driver for shock but they couldn't find anything wrong with my boyfriend or me. I didn't have so much as a scratch on me and no signs of whiplash from the impact. But looking at the car, I knew the policeman was right and that we should by rights have been dead.

Lisa came to see me after the accident and we talked about what it had meant. She had no doubt that her father had saved her life by cushioning her boyfriend and her during the impact. I told her I have often heard people describe that feeling of floating as if you are being held by angelic arms. I've experienced it myself and even though I work with spirit every day of my life, I still find it uncanny.

Lisa realised she was being given a second chance but that she had to start taking more care of herself. She'd been driving that sports car of hers far too fast and she could have killed not only herself but her boyfriend as well. She had to slow down – literally and metaphorically – and start living her life more consciously instead of rushing headlong from one experience to the next.

The Final Visit

In the last moments of our lives, we are never alone. Someone who has gone before will always come to collect us, whether it's a grandparent, a parent, a partner, a child or a good friend. If you have ever sat with someone who is dying, you will know that an incredible calmness comes over them because they have seen or heard the person they love coming for them. Many, many people have described this to me and I know we will all go through it one day. There is nothing to fear at that moment, and the dying know it. All will be well.

To illustrate this, I'm including a story I heard from a doctor about an end-of-life and after-life experience he had.

One evening I was called out to the home of a fifty-four-year-old woman who had a history of heart problems. When I walked into her bedroom I was surprised to see so many people there and asked them to leave so I could examine my patient in peace. Her husband and two daughters left the room, but a man and a woman still stood in the corner, smiling.

'Would you mind stepping out for a moment?' I asked, getting irritated, but all they did was smile.

My patient was very weak but she managed to say: 'It's only you and me in the room, doctor. The lady and gentleman you can see are my parents and they've come for me because it's my time to die.'

'Nonsense,' I said. 'You're not going to die if I've got anything to do with it.' But when I did my examination, I realised her heart was very weak and that she must have had another heart attack. I called an ambulance and waited with her until it came.

'My mother died at forty-seven,' she told me, 'and my dad took his own life a year later. They haven't appeared to me since then – until now. That's why I know I'm going to die and they will take me over.'

The family went with her to hospital and I popped in later to find them all sitting round her bedside as she got weaker and weaker. She told them that she had left letters for all of them that they were to read after she died. They talked about her funeral requests. Then, two hours later, she passed away with a beautiful smile on her face.

Just after that, I heard her voice in my head. 'You are free now, free to look after the ones you love.' The words were clear and unmistakable and they made me stop in my tracks.

I was so moved by the whole experience that it changed my whole approach to medicine. Now, when I am with a dying patient, I know they are about to be set free from suffering, and I know that they will go on to an afterlife. I have no doubt about it any more, having actually heard from a patient of mine after her death.

I have died myself, as I will describe in chapter 7, and I can vouch for the fact that there is nothing to fear. In fact, it felt so beautiful and natural that I was disappointed when I realised that I would have to come back again! I still find it uncanny – and wonderful – that angels look after us at every stage of the journey. In the next chapter, we will look at encounters with angels we haven't met in this lifetime, who come to us for a reason.

Chapter 3

Angels We Don't Recognise

There are many kinds of angels that look out for us at different times. There are the angels who are sent to guide us when we are children – like my lovely man in the brown suit. There are close family members and friends who have passed over and come back to keep an eye on us, as we discussed in the last chapter. Different angels guide us as adults because the problems and decisions we face change and we need different kinds of guidance. There are souls who knew us in one or more of our past lives who come back to keep an eye on us as spirit guides. There are special angels who walk the earth in human form. And we all have a main guardian angel who keeps us safe, a soul who is so evolved that it has never had an earthly life. There may be times when we feel alone, but we never are. None of us walk alone in this world. In fact, there's usually quite a crowd around!

The image of angels that those of us brought up in a Christian faith are familiar with is of a male figure in white with feathered wings and a halo. I haven't seen an angel like this myself but I've spoken to many people who have, and I have felt a sensation that was just like soft, feathered wings wrapped around me at a time when I was very depressed. I felt totally safe and enclosed and I knew it was an angel but I didn't need to know any more. I felt comforted and reassured, and realised that's why that angel came to me at that particular time.

I should explain here that I am not a member of any church. I believe in God and Jesus Christ, but I don't like the dogma of the church, and some priests and vicars I have met left me cold because I felt they were approaching their role as a job rather than a vocation. I'm not against religion. I love empty churches, because I can feel in them the love of all the people that have come together there. But I don't need to worship in a church to feel close to God, because I feel close to him all the time.

The God I believe in isn't the humanised character with long wavy hair depicted in children's Bibles. I believe God is an energy, a force that it is very hard for human beings to comprehend. However, I have seen Christ and he did look something like the image with which we are all familiar in great art and sculpture from across the ages.

I was doing a reading for an ex-nun. She'd lived in a convent most of her life before deciding that she wanted to get out and see the world before she died. Just after I started the reading, a light came into the room from high up. I had my eyes closed but I knew the light was there, followed by a shimmering blue outline. I opened one eye and saw a curl of brown hair just in front of me.

'Who are you?' I asked.

The head inclined and I saw it was a man. 'I am the Christ,' he said.

I opened both eyes and my first thought was that he wore the cross on his face because he had straight eyebrows and a straight nose forming a cross shape, as well as beautiful olive skin and eyes that you could drown in. Then I noticed that his hands were out-stretched and there were blue-white beams of light coming from his palms and shining into me. This all happened in seconds and I felt as though I had been lit up. I felt an incredible sense of love and awe and I sat for a moment or two trying to gather my thoughts.

The nun asked me, 'What have you just seen? What have you experienced?'

I told her what had happened, then said, 'He must have come for you.'

'Oh no, my dear,' she said. 'He came for you. I didn't see him.' And she smiled at me. 'What a very special gift.'

We became friends, that lady and I, and I found out that she is one of the angels who walk the earth. She is one of the most profound people I have ever met. The sense of bliss I felt that day during the reading I gave her is something that has never left me. I can still feel it in times of need – not exactly the same, but a sense memory of the feeling that brings comfort in itself.

When I do readings for clients, I often get the spirits of loved ones who have passed over, and they are all angels who come with the intent of bringing comfort and advice. But a few times in my life I have had an encounter with a pure angel during a reading and it's quite an amazing feeling.

A famous man, who I can't name for reasons of confidentiality, came to me after his young son died. He blamed himself for the death, because he had been unable to protect his boy, and he sat in front of me totally broken. All of a sudden a light came from within me – that's the only way I can describe it – and I heard words being spoken to this man, in my voice, but they were not my words. They were so profound that he sat mesmerised, unable to move, throughout the whole experience.

After it was over, the man said, 'I feel as though I can start getting on with my life now. I know without any doubt that my son is in a good place.'

He is not a religious man, but what the angel said through me had touched him to his core. Unfortunately

I can't remember much of it. When I am channelling for a spirit I can hear everything I am saying and usually I am consciously repeating what they tell me. But when it is a pure angel speaking, they aren't using my words at all. They don't use my vocabulary. There is a different presence in the room and it is a wonderful, calm feeling, very blissful, like all the good things in the world rolled into one.

So there are different levels of angels. Many of you reading this may be angels without wings here on earth. You know if you are a good person or not. Do you spontaneously help those in need without any thought of reward? I'm sure you can think of people in your life who are kind and generous with their time, and without realising it, these people are 'earning their wings'.

Seeing the Light

When guardian angels come into our lives, it is often quite a dramatic experience, one that you will never forget. That's what happened to me on the clifftop when the two pairs of angelic hands lifted me back from almost certain death and deposited me out of harm's way on the other side of a barbed wire fence. After it happened, there was no question in my mind that it must have been angels. There was no other explanation. And so it was with Simon, a young student who came to see me and told me about his angelic experience.

I was walking home from university listening to my iPod, with the earphones in my ears, but I wasn't in a dream world. I was still perfectly aware of my surroundings. Anyway, I got to a road, looked both ways and the coast was clear so I stepped out onto the tarmac to cross. Suddenly there was a brilliant light blinding me, so bright I couldn't see anything at all. I stopped abruptly and at that point I felt a whoosh of air as a large vehicle whizzed past. It all happened in a split second.

The bright light vanished, I looked to my left and realised I had narrowly missed being hit by a double-decker bus that was travelling at speed. Then I looked down and realised I was back on the pavement. Now, I know for a fact that I had stepped off that pavement with both feet, but looking back I remember a feeling of being pushed backwards. It happened so fast that I thought at first I must have imagined it. But in retrospect, I know for certain that it happened. I can clearly remember the sensation of a pressure that forced me back to safety.

I felt as though something very special happened to me that day. It changed my life in many ways. I think I was helped for a reason and it made me change my mind about what I want to do when I graduate. Rather than pursue research studies, I want to go out into the world and help other people. The whole experience definitely made me a more spiritual person.

I've heard many people describe a bright light in front of them. It fills their field of vision, and there is a fuzzy halo at the edges, like looking into the sun. I believe that angels put that light in front of you when you are not listening. It's their way of getting your attention with an oomph! They'd probably been trying to pre-warn Simon but he was too busy with his music and it needed a more dramatic intervention to stop him walking under that bus.

A Mother's Story

I hear many stories of angelic interventions to prevent fatal road accidents. I suppose it is because that is the most common cause of early death in the Western world, where we don't have killer diseases like malaria, and most of us have good sanitation and access to healthy food. Almost all of us will be in a car accident at some point in our life, whether as drivers, passengers or pedestrians, and often it is only a hair's breadth that makes the difference between walking away scot-free, and serious injury or death. I believe angels are often involved in making that difference.

I was late arriving at school to pick up my eleven-year-old son Charlie, and when I got there, there were no parking spaces left on the playground side of the road. I pulled into a space on the other side and got out of the car, scanning the crowds of children to pick out my son's blond curls. We saw each other at the same time, waved, and then suddenly he sprinted out between two parked cars and into the road towards me. I saw a car coming from the left and screamed 'Stop!' I waved my arms in the air frantically but the car was almost upon him and I froze with sick, helpless fear, my worst nightmare about to be enacted right in front of my eyes.

I heard a scream – not mine – and then I blinked and the car had gone past. I looked for his body on the road but couldn't see it then I realised that somehow my son was back on the pavement.

'Stay there!' I shouted, and ran across the road to grab him in a big hug, my heart beating so hard I thought I was going to collapse. He seemed a bit dazed and just hugged me back. Then I realised that another mother was leaning against the playground fence looking almost as shocked as I was.

'He was lifted,' she said, her voice shaky. 'There was nobody there but he was lifted into the air and put back on the pavement. I was right here and saw it as clear as day.'

'That's true,' my son said. 'I couldn't see anyone but I could feel these hands holding me. It felt like someone very strong.'

Later that day, at bedtime, Charlie said to me. 'Do you know what, Mum? I think it was Jesus who saved my life today.'

Whoever it was, I am eternally grateful to them. I still feel shaky when I think back to that moment when I nearly lost my son.

Of course, many teenagers do die in road accidents. It's the most common cause of death in British teens, and if you have lost a child in this way, you may wonder why yours wasn't saved while Charlie and many others were. I can only say that that is how it was meant to be. Some people have very short lives because they have fulfilled whatever their purpose was supposed to be in this lifetime. When children die, they are at the end of their life cycles and have evolved into the purest form of angel. You often hear relatives describing them as an angel, although they may not realise how true it actually is. It's terrible for their parents, of course, but it is part of their life plan to learn from the experience in some way so that their souls evolve.

As a parent I've had a number of narrow escapes myself. My daughter Nicky was fifteen when a friend of hers who had recently passed his driving test asked her if she would like to come for a day out with him and a couple of their other friends. Nicky liked and trusted the boy and was all set to go, thinking it would be a lot of fun, but at the last minute a little voice in her head warned her not to get in the car. She's her mother's daughter and knows to listen to 'little voices' so reluctantly she told her friends that she wasn't coming after all and would meet up with them later.

That car hit a tree and all three of the teenagers inside were killed. A guardian angel had spared Nicky by warning her not to go. It was desperately sad for her attending the funerals of her friends and thinking about what might have been, and it still disturbs both of us to this day.

That's not the only time Nicky has been saved from harm. On 17 December 1983, she was on her way to Harrods to meet a friend for coffee when a voice in her head told her 'You mustn't go. Stay away.' She managed to phone and warn the friend not to go either and, that evening, they were both badly shaken when they saw on the news that an IRA bomb had gone off outside Harrods, killing six people and injuring seventy-five.

Then there was another incident when my son Carl decided to have a party for his eighteenth birthday and invited all his friends. Out of the blue, Nicky told him

'Andrew shouldn't come on his motorbike. Make sure he doesn't.'

Andrew didn't have a big powerful motorbike – just a little white moped. 'Why on earth not?' Carl asked.

'If he comes on his bike, he will have an accident at a roundabout,' Nicky told him firmly.

Carl was a bit scathing. 'Who told you that then?'

'My angel,' she said, and she was so convincing that finally Carl rang Andrew and told him not to come on his bike.

So Andrew got a lift to the party and it all went well, but the very next day he wanted to pop round to see Carl about something and he decided to hop on his bike. After all, Nicky's warning had only covered the day of the party. As he approached the only roundabout on the route, her words came into his head and he slowed down to a safe speed, just in case. And thank goodness he did! As he turned into the roundabout, suddenly his back wheel came loose and fell off, and he skidded to a halt on the grass verge.

Andrew was really shaken when he got to our house. 'I looked at the road and there was nothing there that could have caused the wheel to come off. It was a completely inexplicable accident. But if I hadn't been driving very carefully because of Nicky's warning, I could have been very badly hurt.'

Nowadays Nicky's friends don't bother to ask for a reason. If she says they shouldn't go somewhere or do something, they always follow her advice.

All for the Sake of a Chainsaw

Like Nicky, a woman I know called Catherine listened to her instincts and prevented an accident that seemed likely to happen.

I had a dream one night about a man and a girl riding a motorbike, both dressed in black leathers and with helmets covering their faces. I live across the lane from a wildlife park which has a long, tree-lined drive and I could see the bike coming up this drive in my dream, when suddenly the girl fell off the back. When I woke the next morning, I just couldn't get the dream out of my head and I decided that I probably shouldn't go on my partner Richard's motorbike that day.

However, my car was outside my sister's house five miles away because we'd been there for dinner the night before and got a taxi back. Also, Richard found that the chain had snapped on his chainsaw and he would have to take it into town to get it fixed. As far as he was concerned, it made sense for him to drive into town on his motorbike with me on the back, so he went to the shed and brought it out and started the engine.

A voice in my head was crying 'No, no, no!' I knew Richard wouldn't be swayed from his plans by 'voices in my head', so I went over to have a look at the bike and noticed that the back tyre was so bald, the metal was showing through. It looked like an accident waiting to happen, but Richard still wanted to go. I had to think of another way to dissuade him.

Then an idea came into my head. Our friend Ben who worked in the wildlife park had a chainsaw so I ran over and told him what had happened, asking if we could borrow his saw to save Richard the journey. Not only did he lend me his saw, but he also gave me his car keys so that Richard and I could pick up the car in safety.

After that, I persuaded Richard to fix the tyre on the bike and sell it. I felt that the angels had been working with me that day to prevent an accident, and it was up to me to work with them as well if I wanted my luck to hold.

When Catherine told me this story, I had to agree with her. She was getting one warning after another and it would have been crazy to ignore them. However, angels can still rescue us from serious harm even if we continually ignore their warnings. Sometimes they can overrule us and save us from ourselves. It all depends if it's in our life blueprint.

Car with a Built-in Parachute

Caroline was driving to her boyfriend's house, which was along a narrow lane in Cornwall. As was her way, she was driving too fast and when she came to a particularly sharp bend she lost control of the car.

It went up the bank and flipped over, but it all happened very slowly, as if in slow motion. The car rolled over twice and ended up with the driver's side down on the road. The passenger window had smashed so I crawled up through it and got out onto the verge, a bit shaken but totally unharmed.

I stood looking at the car, unable to believe my luck. I hadn't been wearing a seatbelt so it's incredible that I hadn't got a serious head injury when it rolled over. I know this sounds weird but I felt as though the car had been held in someone's hands and placed gently down on the road. Or as if it had a parachute attached so that there was a soft landing.

A person in a nearby house had heard the crash and phoned the emergency services. My boyfriend and his brother heard there had been an accident and came to check it wasn't me – and of course it was.

'Are you sure you're OK?' they kept saying. 'How on earth did you walk away from that without a scratch?'

They seemed more shaken by it all than I was at the time.

I should have had terrible injuries, but I believe I was saved by an angel, and now I always carry a little angel charm with me wherever I go.

I know several people who carry angel charms and if it brings them comfort and helps them to focus on their angels, that's a good thing. You don't need a charm to get their help, though. They are with us all the time anyway. Most of the time you don't need to do anything; they will take care of us without any acknowledgement at all.

The Car That Was Lifted

Here's another very dramatic angel rescue told to me by a woman called Sandra, that was witnessed by several people at the scene on a big interstate highway in the American Midwest.

I was driving to the mall with my small son strapped into his car seat in the back. The roads were quiet that mid-morning, with the rush hour long past. Suddenly I saw a huge truck that had toppled onto its side and was hurtling towards us at speed. I pressed my foot hard on the brake pedal but the truck was still coming at us, like something out of a horror movie, and I screamed 'Oh my God, we're going to die!' There was nothing I could do to avoid it.

Just as the truck reached us, my car was lifted up into the air, over the truck, and placed on the road on the other side. It must have happened quickly but to me it felt as though it was in slow motion. The truck continued skidding down the freeway and came to a stop a hundred yards beyond us, but some drivers on the other side pulled over and came to have a word with me where I sat shaking convulsively in my seat.

'Are you guys OK? What on earth just happened there?' one asked.

'Does your car have super-powers?' another said, amazed. 'You just flew over that truck.'

And a woman smiled at me and said, 'You were saved by angels. Your lives were meant to continue today, not end.'

I turned to hug my little boy, but he was playing with his action figures, oblivious to everything that had happened.

Sandra spoke to the truck driver later on, and he was in shock – not just from his own accident but also because of the sight of a car flying right over him at the point when he was sure he was going to smash into them. He was saved as well, because if he had collided with

Sandra's car, the impact could have caused his truck to explode. No one was meant to die there that day. Everyone who witnessed the 'flying car' was profoundly shaken up and I'm sure all their beliefs have been influenced by it.

Angels Helping as We Drive

I know of several instances where drivers have been given sufficient warning to prevent accidents. Sometimes the angels just take control of the car, as in the case of Emily, a teacher who lives in Kent.

I was driving on my usual route to work one morning when all of a sudden my leg was forced to press hard on the brake pedal. I didn't have control of my own muscles at that moment as my foot was pushed down to the floor and the car jerked to a standstill. A fraction of a second later, another car came rushing round a bend up ahead on my side of the road. The driver had been overtaking and only just managed to cut back onto his own side with inches to spare. I hadn't seen or heard him coming but if my car hadn't stopped when it did we would have had a head-on collision. I felt a strong sense that an angel had rescued me that day.

Something similar happened to Avril, a client of mine in the United States.

> I was driving home along the I-90 after organising a large convention when I fell asleep at the wheel of the car. I only woke up when the car hit a bush and came to a standstill. I looked around and realised with horror that I was on the wrong side of the interstate. Somehow I had crossed the central reservation and got through the oncoming traffic on the other side. What's more, the carriageways are separated by thick trees at that stage and my car had driven through the only gap for miles around.
>
> As I sat checking myself for injuries (there weren't any), I suddenly remembered a voice talking to me in my dreams. It said 'You're safe now.' And I realised that an angel had taken control of my car when I fell asleep and had guided it to safety.

Sometimes a voice tells drivers to stop and they are able to react in time. Here's Rosalind's story.

> I stopped at a crossroads and looked left, right, left, then put my foot on the accelerator to pull out when all of a sudden a voice in my head said 'Stop!' I didn't recognise the voice but it sounded authoritative, so I just stopped. It was almost an automatic reaction. And a fraction of a

second later a car appeared out of nowhere and crossed directly in front of me at speed. I truly hadn't seen it and if I hadn't heard the voice saying 'stop', it would definitely have hit me. I'm a more cautious driver now, and I always avoid that particular crossroads.

Sometimes the angelic message can be even more specific than just the word 'stop'.

I'd been out for the evening with three friends of mine and was driving home in the dark along a narrow, twisting country road. I wasn't speeding but I was doing a good thirty miles an hour, when I heard the words 'Badger, stop!' in my head, and somehow I knew that if I didn't stop I would hit a badger. I put my foot on the brake and managed to come to a halt just as I reached a bend, and there ahead of me I saw the distinctive white stripe caught in my headlights as a badger ambled across the road and into the bushes.

If I hadn't stopped, I would either have hit and killed it, or I would have swerved and had an accident myself. But why did the word 'badger' come into my head, and not 'deer' or 'rabbit', since they are much more common sights on the roads round my Cornwall home? Badgers are pretty rare, and I'm incredibly grateful that I didn't kill one.

I've heard many times of people getting a feeling that they shouldn't drive on a particular day, or having a sense of foreboding about a journey. Women seem to have a keener sense for these warnings than men. They either listen to the feeling and stay at home, or they set out anyway and have an accident or come close to one.

It might not be a 'feeling' or a voice. Angels will use whichever method they think will be most effective to get through to you, so make sure you remain alert to warnings. Remember: you could be a hair's breadth away from a serious accident every time you take your car out.

Taking Your Own Life

I have never judged people who take their own lives, or try to do so. My Uncle Charlie put his head in a gas oven when I was ten years old, so it was a concept I was familiar with from an early age. We have many different lifetimes and will all commit suicide in at least one of them. People who are sympathetic to those who attempt suicide have probably done it themselves in one of their past lives, while those who are angry and judgmental about it, or just unable to comprehend, have not been there yet.

Sometimes when we are in the depths of despair, we might come close to suicide but if it is not our moment to die, an angel will step in. Mike's was a tragic story. His wife Doreen got cancer and he gave up his job to nurse her for the last two years of her life. They didn't have children of their own but had taken in a teenage boy called Darren from a very rough part of London to try and help him make a good life. After Doreen died, Darren started going off the rails and Mike found out he was taking drugs. I'll let him tell the story in his own words.

I tried my best to talk to him and offered whatever he wanted if he would just stop the heroin. I really tried, but I kept hitting a brick wall. 'I like it so I'll keep taking it,' he'd say. I knew that he had needed something to keep him going after Doreen died but heroin wasn't the answer. I did everything I could think of but nothing worked and I felt like a complete failure.

I'd gone back to work but it was just a factory job that I did for money, not something I enjoyed. Friends tried to cheer me up but I felt they didn't understand. Gradually, as the first anniversary of Doreen's death drew near, I came to the decision that I had nothing left to live for.

We'd always said that we would leave Darren our money and the house, but I was worried that he would just use it to buy drugs, so I went to a lawyer and changed my will so that there would be enough to look after him in the meantime but he wouldn't get the lump sum until his twenty-first birthday, by which time I hoped he would have got his act together.

On the day I'd decided that I would kill myself, I tidied the house first and dressed myself nicely in a suit and tie. I kept talking to Doreen, telling her that I was coming to join her. When I was ready, I got in the car and drove out to a clifftop some distance from our home town. It was a place we had once gone walking together and really liked, and I chose it because it was remote, but I knew the cliff was high enough that there was no chance I would survive the drop. I planned to push my accelerator foot to the floor and drive very, very fast off the edge.

I had to get the car through a wooden gate and drive across a field, and I stopped ten yards back from the cliff edge to think my final thoughts. 'I'm coming to you now, Doreen,' I said, and at that point I felt a hand on my right shoulder. It was such a clear feeling that I jumped and looked round to see if anyone was there – but they weren't. My own hands were on the steering wheel. Then I felt another hand on my left shoulder and the hands were holding me back in the seat very firmly. The thought popped into my head: 'An angel is holding me.'

I saw an image of my car hurtling over the cliff edge. Then it was as if the camera panned outwards and I could see that the tide was out and there were people on the beach down below just wandering along, picking up pieces of driftwood. It had never occurred to me that I risked taking someone else's life in the process of taking my own. That was the last thing I wanted to do.

I could still feel the hands on my shoulders as I turned the wheel so the car was facing away from the edge. I put the handbrake on, got out, then I sank down on the grass and wept until I didn't have any tears left in me, until I was completely wrung dry. At last I got into the car and drove home.

When I got back, Darren was sitting waiting for me. He leapt up and came running over to give me a hug. 'Dad, I'm so sorry about the drugs. I'm going to stop now. I really want to get clean and I need you to help me. Will you help?'

Now, I am not given to fanciful thoughts but when I looked back on it all later, I realised that it had been an angel's hands holding me back on the clifftop. There was a reason why my life was saved that day, and I believe it was so that I could help Darren to get off drugs, which I'm glad to say he has done now. I still miss my wife very much, but Darren and I have become close and he is a real comfort to me. My life is very different now, and every day I thank the angel who saved me.

When we are born we all take on a personality and with it comes free will. That means that we can choose whether to be a good person in our life or not. Souls don't do that; souls have purity. But human beings can choose to be bad and if they do that, they will get many signs and warnings to change their ways. I haven't spoken to Darren in person but I wonder if an angel helped him to make the decision to come off drugs? It could have been Doreen, the woman he saw as a mother, influencing him from the other side, or it could have been one of the other angels tasked with looking after him.

Angels are around us all the time, but they don't make themselves known unless we really need them – perhaps if we are very depressed and need strength to get us back on our life's path, as Mike was, or perhaps if we are behaving badly and going astray, as Darren was. Bringing comfort in times of need is one of their key roles.

The Missing Handrail

I do regular readings for a woman called Linda, who is about fifty years old and has a very bad back. She slipped a disc some years ago and the vertebrae in her lower back have been fused together, meaning she's not very agile. She walks with difficulty and I know her back begins to ache if she has to sit or stand too long in one position. She works in a florist's shop not far from where I live. Here's her angelic experience, fully corroborated by a witness who saw the whole thing:

A delivery van had just arrived to bring us our fresh flowers for the day. The owner of the shop was busy so she asked me to go out and have a look to see what I thought we could use. Little steps folded down at the back of the van and I climbed into a well at the top of the steps then up to the floor of the van, where I started looking through all the glorious summer blooms: roses, peonies, stocks, lupins, sweetpeas – all my favourites.

The delivery man stood in the back making notes as I listed what we wanted: six of these, twelve of the next, and so forth. I was engrossed in the job, moving from side to side as I examined the blooms, and didn't realise I was near the well. I took a step backwards, lost my balance and toppled over. In that split second I thrust my hand out and grabbed hold of a handrail, managing to stop the fall and pull myself up again.

'Goodness, that was a close one!' I remarked to a driver.

He was open-mouthed with surprise. 'What on earth stopped you falling?' he asked. 'I thought you were a goner.'

'The handrail, of course,' I said. I turned to point to it and it was only then I realised there was no handrail there. But I could still feel the cool metal in my hand. It was strong and solid and it hadn't budged when I grabbed it with one hand and then the other.

I'll never forget that sensation of grabbing a handrail that proved not to be there. If I had fallen out of the back of the lorry, goodness knows how badly my back would have been damaged. I doubt I would have been able to work any more.

Linda knew straight away that she had been saved by an angel. Most people I talked to for this book described a feeling after the events in question that was like 'a deep inner knowing' – a message that is so clear, so succinct, that it clicks somewhere within. Many of them were sceptics before – particularly the men, who usually want to find 'rational' or 'technical' explanations for everything. But I suspect that even they would be stumped by the case of the missing handrail!

A Different Way Home

Jeremy was a young man who would definitely have put himself in the 'sceptical' camp until the following incident occurred.

I was walking home one autumn evening after a night out with friends at the cinema. I was thinking about the film we'd just seen, and about the girlfriend troubles one of my friends had been having, and all of a sudden a voice came into my head: 'Take another way home. It's not safe.'

I was just about to turn down a road lined by blocks of flats that led almost directly to my home but the voice had been so strong and definite that I hesitated. The road looked particularly dimly lit and I could see that at least one of the lampposts wasn't illuminated. But on the other hand, it was by far the quickest way home and I had walked along it almost every night since moving to that area. Now, I'm not superstitious and I'm almost embarrassed to admit that I listened to 'a voice in my head', but I decided on a whim to take another route just for that one night. I got home ten minutes later, berating myself for being an idiot, and went to bed.

The next morning I switched on the local radio station to listen to the news while I made my breakfast. The newsreader said there had been a stabbing in the area the night before and that police were appealing for witnesses. He said that if anyone had been in such and such a road (the one I had decided not to turn down) at around 11 pm (exactly the time I was there) they should contact the police in case they had witnessed anything.

I sat staring at the radio with my spoon held in mid air for at least a minute! I could still hear that voice in my head saying, 'Take another way home'. I've got no idea who it was, but I can only think it must have been an angel. Just don't tell anyone I said so!

I've changed 'Jeremy's' name because he didn't want to be identified. A few other people whose stories are in this book made the same request. Personally, I think you should share the news when angels visit you. It's a great blessing, and I think it's a shame that some people are embarrassed to admit it.

The Gap on the Subway

I don't normally tell strangers I meet about what I do for a living. Everyone needs time off. But sometimes I meet people who seem so open and spiritual that I find myself telling them that I work as a medium and in those instances, they often come out with stories of their own experiences with spirits and angels. When I meet someone in an unusual way, I find there's usually a reason for it.

The first time I visited New York, I told the cab driver who picked me up at the airport it was my first visit and he offered to give me a guided tour of some of the sights tourists don't normally see. He took me to places like Grand Central Station and we were getting on so well that he turned off the meter so we could chat. It was almost lunchtime and when he heard I didn't have lunch plans he asked if I would like to come to his friend's restaurant nearby, and I agreed.

When we got there, I was introduced to the manager and a couple of the staff came over to sit with us. I hadn't mentioned what I did for a living, but they started talking about spirit themselves. And one of the waiters, who was the son of the manager, told me the following story:

I was waiting for the subway in rush hour. I don't know if you've been down there but it's packed six-deep on the platform so that when the crowd moves you have to move as well. The train pulled in and the crowd surged forward to get on. I found myself at the front, with a door opening straight ahead of me, and I was about to step forwards when I head a voice in my head saying, 'Careful, feet,' and there was a pressure on my chest as if someone or something was pushing me backwards.

I looked down and there was a gap about a foot wide between the platform and the train and I just hadn't seen it. Gaps like that are very rare on the New York subway but the platform curved in this station and that was the result. I could have been seriously hurt if I had stepped into that gap. As it was, I managed to step over it and warn everyone behind me to be careful as well. I truly believe it was an angel who warned me and stopped me getting hurt that day.

I told him that I totally agreed and that's when I explained what I did for a living. I also told him that one day I would write a book about angels coming to help us, and asked if he minded if I included his story in it.

'I'd be honoured,' he said.

I don't often let myself be taken for lunch with a group of strangers but when it feels right, there's usually a reason for the connection. They always turn out to be like-minded people.

Neighbourhood Watch – with a Difference

When a crime is prevented by angelic intervention, the angels can work in several different ways. They might persuade the criminal to turn back; they might alert the police to the criminal's intentions; or they might warn the potential victim to take more care. I've come across all these circumstances (and I'll tell you more about my work with the police force both here and in the US in chapter 4). Perhaps there was a mixture of all three circumstances going on in the following story, told to me by an elderly widow called Patricia.

I was woken up one night by a voice in my head. 'Go and close the hall window', it said. I was sure I had closed that window earlier and was still very drowsy so I just ignored it and went back to sleep again. I remember the clock said 2.14 am.

Twenty minutes later, at 2.34 am, I was woken again by the voice saying, 'Go and close the hall window.'

'Oh, for goodness' sake!' I thought crossly. 'I suppose I'd better go down and check or I'll never get back to sleep properly.'

I clambered out of bed and down the stairs and realised that I had indeed left a small window in the hall open. It wasn't big enough for anyone to climb through but they could have reached in and opened the bigger window down below and got into my house that way. As I closed the small window and turned the little knob to lock it, a movement caught my eye in the back garden. I saw two dark shapes and realised they were men clambering over my garden wall and onto the lawn.

I'm in my late seventies and live alone, so I was utterly terrified. I crept into the sitting room and crouched down behind the sofa as I dialled 999 and told the police what I had just seen. I remained hidden in there for about fifteen minutes, scared that the intruders might break in. Finally I saw flashing lights outside and heard a knock on the door and the reassuring shout of 'Police!'

When I opened the door, a policewoman told me they had apprehended two men acting suspiciously in next-door's garden, so I could go back to bed without fear. The following day, the police came back and explained to me that the two men they'd arrested as a result of my call had been carrying a laptop computer and a holdall full of valuables from one of my neighbour's houses.

'What were you doing awake and looking out the window at that time of night?' the policewoman asked. 'Do you suffer from insomnia?'

I didn't like to tell her that an angel had wakened me, but I'm positive in my own mind that that's what it was. And I feel very reassured to know that I'm not on my own when I climb the stairs and go to bed at night.

The outcome of this story relied on split-second timing. Patricia got up to close her window just at the moment the burglars climbed into her garden. Any sooner and she wouldn't have seen them; any later and they could have been inside her house. And when the police arrived the burglars were still on the scene with the damning evidence in their hands. I think angels may have been influencing the burglars and the police as well as Patricia for this incident to conclude so neatly.

The Angel at Ground Zero

A lot of men don't ever tell anyone after experiencing an angelic intervention, but I met someone in New York – a taxi driver called Joe – who couldn't help spilling out his story to me. I think in some ways he was still in shock about his experience and looking for someone who could explain it to him. That's probably why I was directed to hail down his cab that spring day.

Joe was a chatty kind of guy anyway, and when he heard my English accent he wanted to know if I was there on vacation and if it was my first time in the city. I explained that I was there to work, giving a seminar for people who wanted to learn how to use their own psychic powers. And that's when his story spilled out.

It was in spring 2002, six months after 9/11, when a woman flagged me down and asked me to take her to the Twin Towers.

'Do you mean Ground Zero?' I asked. Surely there couldn't be anyone on the planet who didn't know about the planes flying into those towers?

'South Tower,' she continued, then said: 'Don't take the direct route. Go by the longest way you possibly can.'

I shrugged and set off on a scenic route, assuming she must be a tourist who wanted to see a bit of the city. I started to chat to her but she was barely responding and I realised she wasn't in the mood for conversation, so after a while I stopped. It occurred to me that maybe she had lost someone when the towers came down and she was going on a pilgrimage to see where it had happened. Maybe that's why she wanted peace and quiet.

My cell phone rang at one stage and I answered it, but the line went dead. Shortly afterwards the radio started crackling like crazy, as if picking up static, but I thought nothing of it.

Just before we reached Ground Zero the woman suddenly spoke.

'You brought me here on my last journey and were particularly nice to me,' she said. 'It's my turn to look out for you now.'

I indicated and slowed down to pull in to a stopping place, and when I turned round, she wasn't there. The cab doors hadn't been opened, because there's a locking system that I have to press to release. I jumped out and looked up and down the street but couldn't see any sign of her. I knew for sure I'd had a woman in my cab. Where on earth was she?

A couple on the sidewalk came over wanting a ride. I asked if they had seen a woman getting out just a minute earlier. They said no, they hadn't. They'd seen me pull over and stop but no one had got out of the cab.

I opened the back door to see if there was any sign of her, but the only thing there was a tiny white feather on the back seat. I shrugged and carried on with my day, but I was feeling very shaken up by the whole incident.

A couple of hours later, I was just going off duty when another driver pulled up alongside me. 'Did you hear about the pile-up on West Street?'

'No.'

He told me there had been at least a dozen cars involved, two people were dead and several others were seriously injured.

All the time he was talking, I was thinking about the fact that I would have been on West Street if that disappearing woman passenger hadn't asked me to take her on the long route to Ground Zero. When he told me the time of the accident, I realised it was exactly the time I would have been there. So that woman guided me away from the area and possibly stopped me being involved in a very nasty accident.

I realised afterwards that I didn't have a very clear memory of her face. I don't know why, because usually I'm good on faces. But the idea came into my head that I had dropped her off at the Twin Towers one morning not long before 9/11 and I think I might have helped her with some heavy bags. And then I began to wonder if maybe she died in the attack on the towers and that it was her ghost who had been in the back of my cab.

Did she save my life? I'll never really know, but since then I keep getting a spooky feeling that she is watching over me and helping out. Before I met her, I'd had a run of rude, argumentative customers and now everyone I meet is nice and generous. Is that a coincidence?

After he finished his story I told him that I am a medium and explained about angels who can come and watch over us. I said I was sure that he was right and that's what it was in his case. It might have been someone he had encountered on earth or it could have been an unknown angel in the back of his cab that day.

I also told him that I've heard many people say they found a feather after an angelic intervention. They're always tiny white downy feathers and they appear in a place you wouldn't expect to see them. I live in the middle of the countryside where there are no white-feathered birds, but I often come across tiny white feathers. One summer's day I had dozed off in a sun lounger out in the garden and woke up to find one white feather on my lap, one by my side, and one in my hand, and I knew for sure I had been visited that day and that the angel responsible wanted me to know it.

We had reached my destination by this time and Joe was looking at me in the mirror of his cab.

'What is it?' I laughed.

'There's something about your eyes,' he said. 'You've got the same eyes as that woman in my cab.'

'Well, it wasn't me,' I promised him. 'I wasn't in New York on 9/11 – although I was supposed to be.'

I'd had a meeting scheduled for the morning of 11 September 2001, not far from the Twin Towers. About a week before, I said to Michael: 'I'm not going. I'm going to cancel the flight.'

He argued with me that the flight was non-refundable, and that it would be difficult to reschedule that meeting, but I insisted. The angels had told me not to go. I didn't know why, but I would do as they said. I managed to change my flight to a few weeks later and rearrange the meeting as well, so I was sitting at home with Michael, watching in horror as the planes flew into the Towers. That's why I had been told not to go.

'So you're psychic,' my taxi driver said thoughtfully. 'Wow, wow, wow!'

He didn't want to take my fare after that, which is unprecedented for a New York cabbie, but I insisted. I could tell he was a good man and he deserved every good thing that happened to him.

In this chapter, I've talked about people being saved from danger by angels, but in the next I'd like to show how angelic interventions can help you to choose the right path in your life, if you listen and watch for the signposts. It's worth doing, because angels' advice can improve your circumstances in all kinds of ways.

—

Chapter 4

Advice from the Angels

The blueprints of our lives are drawn up in the period between lives, when we are pure souls. We map out our own plans, detailing all kinds of things: whether we'll be single, married or divorced; whether we'll have children; what kind of family we will come from; the jobs we'll do; the people we will be friendly with; the challenges we will face; and the way in which we will die. I think of this life plan as a kind of motorway, the main route from A to B, but shooting off it there will be all kinds of little side roads.

We are born with free will, so while we are travelling along the motorway, we may spot a side road that looks interesting and divert onto it to explore. Some people spend a long time on these side roads, and they may get lost and have trouble finding the motorway again. But all the time you are on a side road, you will have a feeling that something is wrong, or missing, or not quite right. Maybe things will keep going badly for you and you don't know why. People often use the words, 'I can't seem to get back on track.' And they're right – they are literally off track.

How do you make decisions about changing your life? People talk about following their gut instincts, or their intuition, or their better judgement, or they just get 'a strong feeling' about what they should do. I think in all these instances they are being guided by spirit guardians, the angels that watch over our lives and help us to make the right choices. You may feel that you have just had an original, inspired idea – but as far as I'm concerned, that idea was put in your head by a spirit guide. They have many ingenious ways of getting us to pick up on new ideas.

Of course, you can choose to ignore your 'better judgement'. We all do it. I knew I shouldn't have agreed to the way our catering company was being run back in the late 1970s. I didn't want to sign the documents but my husband argued that we were so busy we didn't have time to find another solution. I knew from the start it was a mistake, yet I still allowed it to happen despite the warning voices, and after six months our business had gone. We've all done it. We can ignore our spirit guides, but all the time we are on the wrong side road, they will be niggling away at us in some way, trying to nudge us back onto the motorway again.

Each of us has a spirit guide, someone who has known and watched over us through several different lifetimes. One of my main guides is a Chinese philosopher. I was a student of his, although I don't think I ever graduated. He's never been a member of my family in any lifetime but he has always been there for me. He doesn't reincarnate any more because he has reached a higher level, and that's why I am able to turn to him for advice when I need it – or he can offer advice when I'm not aware that I need it but I actually do! His advice can be very practical, and he doesn't always give reasons for it, but I know to follow it now, and my husband Mike is used to it as well.

We were living just outside Oxford, running a very successful pub, when I was on my own in the kitchen one day and got a message that we should move to Devon. No reasons were given, no explanation offered, but I knew the advice was from my Chinese philosopher.

I went up to the bar and just came out with it straight. 'Michael, we've got to move to Devon. We have to do it.'

He groaned. 'But we've not been here long. Are you sure?'

I said, 'Yes, I'm sure.'

'We'll lose money if we move.'

'We have to go,' I repeated. And it's proof yet again that I married the right man, because he took my word for it and we moved to Devon. (Of course, I already knew I'd married the right man because of the way we met, and the strong messages I got from all my angels at the time.)

As soon as we arrived in Devon I knew it was a good move. There is a good energy there that works for both of us. I started to give more and more readings to friends, and friends of friends, and I was getting very strong guidance that I should work with spirit professionally. It was still another two years before I could bring myself to charge for a reading but moving to Devon was a step in the right direction. It took me closer to finding out what my life's purpose was supposed to be.

Messages from spirit guides, or angels, can be delivered in several different ways – some quite subtle and others completely 'in your face', for people who might not have picked up the subtle hints. I've collected some different types of examples in this chapter.

Fly Canada

A professional photographer called Nigel came to me for a reading because he knew he wanted to change his life but he couldn't decide how. Straight away the word 'Canada' came into my head and at the same time I saw an image of him coming off a cliff face – not falling, but jumping, with a parachute on his back.

'Have you ever done any sky-diving?' I asked him.

'Yes, it's my hobby,' he replied. 'I love it.'

'Well, you're supposed to go to Canada,' I told him. 'You'll have a great life there and it will have something to do with skydiving.'

'Canada?' he repeated, puzzled. 'But I've never thought of going to Canada before. Isn't it a bit cold in winter?'

'Yes, but think of all the beautiful landscapes and wide open spaces,' I said, because that's what I could see in my head.

I could tell that Nigel wasn't convinced as he left, but he looked thoughtful. I'll let him take up the story:

As I drove home from the reading, I suddenly noticed a huge advertising hoarding that I'd never seen before, although I drove along that road every single day, and on that hoarding, in big letters, it said 'Fly Canada'. There were beautiful lakes and forests in the background, exactly the kind of thing I like photographing.

Next morning, I heard the post clattering through the letterbox and went to pick it up. On the top there was a piece of junk mail with the word 'Canada' written in large letters on the envelope. 'Weird,' I thought.

Then later that day, in an idle moment (one of the reasons I wanted to change my life – there wasn't enough work around), I switched on the TV. Believe it or not, there was a programme on about Canada.

'OK, I get the message,' I grinned.

I started exploring possible work for photographers in Canada and it wasn't long before I came across an advert looking for an experienced photographer who could also skydive, for a company that wanted lots of aerial landscape photos. I got in touch and they offered me the job and it's just fantastic. I take footage for movies now as well as stills for advertisements, books and magazines. It's a wonderful life – and I'd never in a million years have considered Canada if it wasn't for all those messages, one after the other.

Angels can't design advertising hoardings or send you junk mail or make television programmes appear, but they can awaken your awareness of them. You might be walking along the street and suddenly a bus goes past with a message on the side, or a name will keep cropping up in lots of different contexts, or a tune will be playing on the radio, or you'll switch on the TV at random and there it will be again. Maybe you'll bump into someone who immediately starts talking about the subject. When this happens, I advise you to listen, and take heed. It could change your life.

An Enforced Career Change

If you are in the wrong job, things will keep going wrong until you sit up and take notice. I hope they never go as badly wrong for you as they did for Clive, the carpenter in this story.

I was making a cabinet one day when I heard a voice in my head telling me to put down the electric saw. I couldn't think of a reason why, so I ignored it and carried on. Three more times I heard the voice saying 'Put down the saw', but it seemed stupid so I kept on working. Shortly after this, one of my clients came in to talk about an order and I shouted to him over the noise of the saw that I'd be with him in just a minute. As I shouted, I felt a terrible pain in my hand and looked down to see that I had completely severed my left thumb. Blood was spurting everywhere.

'You stupid fool!' I thought. Usually I was very careful when working with an electric saw because they are so powerful they can slice through metal as easily as if it were a pound of butter.

The client helped me to wrap my thumb in ice and drove me to hospital but the surgeon was unable to re-attach it because it had been too badly damaged. When I looked back, I realised it had been my dad's voice warning me to put down the saw. We had been very close up to his death three years ago and I'm furious with myself that I didn't listen to him.

I couldn't continue to work as a carpenter with only one thumb and I decided that I would have a go at writing the novel I had been thinking about for some time. I wrote it and, amazingly, found a publisher, and it was so successful when it came out that they commissioned me to write more. I'm now on my fourth novel and I love writing, so the career change was a good thing from that point of view. But I still wish I could get my thumb back!

It doesn't matter whether you recognise the voice you hear or not. Obey first and ask questions later!

Meeting Your Life Partner

Most of us travel down quite a few side roads before meeting the person we are meant to spend our lives with, and it's easy to take the wrong direction. All I can say is that the right one comes along when you least expect it, and maybe when you are not even looking for anyone. Watch out for the signs. Maybe there's a party you have more or less decided not to go to. You're tired, not in the mood, or perhaps there's a good film on the TV. But something keeps nagging at you. You look at the address of the party and it's in a road with a name that's the same as your grandmother's maiden name; you open your wardrobe door and notice an outfit you'd forgotten you had that would be perfect if you did go; and then a friend phones and offers to give you a lift. After all that urging, you'd be crazy not to go.

Then, when you get talking to someone, pay attention if you seem to have lots of random things in common: a love of *Star Trek*, or cheesy puffs, or the colour purple. He or she might not look like the person you imagined in your dreams. They might not have as much money, or such a glamorous job, but if you feel as though they are being thrown into your path somehow, then there is always a reason.

I once did a reading for a woman called Jackie and I was told that she was going to meet her life partner soon. He would have foreign blood, a little bit of grey in his hair and seemingly he already lived round the corner from her. But the spirits warned me that it could all turn on a sixpence – that's the exact phrase they used. I passed all this on to Jackie. Here's what happened next.

A man called Iain came to work at the college where I teach in Exeter. I thought he was a bit odd at first glance and didn't get into conversation with him at all, but one day I had problems with a new computer and asked in the staff room if anyone could help.

'You need either Stuart or Iain,' was the suggestion from my colleague. She checked her mobile and she didn't have Stuart's number – only Iain's. I took it and rang to ask him for help.

Iain came round to my office and soon had the computer up and running, then he went out of his way to be helpful, loading new software and firewall systems that would make my life much easier. He refused to take any money for the work he'd done, so I invited him round for supper as a way of saying 'thank you'.

We had a pleasant conversation over supper but still I didn't think anything more of it until he was leaving and I went to give him a goodnight hug. Suddenly a bolt of lightning shot through me and I felt an intense attraction to him. In my head there was a loud voice saying 'This is your partner on this road', and I realised it must be an angel speaking.

Everything fell into place. I noticed that Iain had a little bit of grey in his hair. He mentioned that he lived round the corner from me. And what's more, he is Scottish, which counts as foreign blood down in the south of England where I come from. All the signs that Dorothy had told me to watch out for were there.

Iain is quite a lot younger than me and I didn't want a toy boy so I remained cautious throughout the early stages of the relationship, but I soon realised it's a true, equal partnership in every sense of the word. Our families get on well, and all my friends like him. It turns out that, far from being new, he'd actually been working at the college for over a year and we hadn't run into each other. We never would have if the angels hadn't brought us together.

It took a lot of coaxing to get Jackie to realise what was right under her nose. There was the message I passed on; her computer problems, and the fact that her colleague only happened to have Iain's number, not Stuart's; then the powerful attraction and angelic words in her head after dinner. It really did turn on a sixpence, but she got there in the end, and they are still very happy together.

It's not just love affairs that can start with messages from angels. If you meet someone as a friend and you become aware that there are a number of coincidences that link you – maybe you both knew the same person at college, or you discovered you'd been at the Taj Mahal on the same day five years ago, or that their partner actually works for the same company as your partner – then it means that you need to be friends with this person because they are going to help you in some way. You may not fully understand how they will help you at the time, but when you look back with hindsight, it will usually become clear.

Of course, as well as telling us who we should be with, angels often warn us about the people we shouldn't be with.

When Not to Marry

Angels will try to protect you when you are with the wrong person so that you don't waste your time. They will draw your awareness to little things and put doubts in your head. These are just little nudges and you might choose to ignore them for a long time, but eventually they will all add up. If a partner is telling lies, angels will plant the word 'lies' in your head. They'll put words in front of you, such as the title of a newspaper article that says 'Beware'. You might not even read the rest of the article but that word 'beware' has entered your consciousness. Your energy will be directed towards the partner's negative qualities. Nobody is making up your mind for you, because you have free will, but eventually so many doubts will creep into your head that you will come to a decision.

A lady called Grace explained to me why she cancelled her wedding just a week before the big day.

We'd known each other for a year, but after he asked me to marry him I went into a mad frenzy of guest lists and menus and I felt as though I never had a moment to myself to stop and think. One day, I told him I was going to the florist's to discuss the flowers I'd chosen and he said he would like to come along with me.

When we got there, the florist had some of my chosen flowers in stock – my favourite stargazer lilies, with the gorgeous dark pink pattern on soft white petals.

'Eww, yuck,' my fiancé exclaimed. 'Are you really going to have these?'

'Yes, they're my favourite flower,' I said, feeling a bit hurt.

'I hate the smell. You'll have to choose something else, because you can't have these.'

It wasn't the fact that he didn't like lilies; it was the way he was telling me what I could or couldn't have on my wedding day that made the hairs stand up on the back of my neck.

'You can't tell me what I can or can't have!' I argued.

'Put it this way: if I knew you had lilies in your bouquet, I wouldn't be turning up at the church.'

I felt as though he had slapped me across the face. Suddenly I got a feeling that he didn't love me enough or he would have let me have the flowers I wanted. But I agreed to change them, and we went home again.

With three weeks to go before the wedding, he looked over my shoulder at the seating plan and said, 'We've got far too many people coming from your side of the family. You need to cut back to just immediate family.'

I was horrified. 'I can't un-invite people I've already invited.'

'Just tell them you're sorry but we've miscalculated and we're short of space.'

I saw that he was adamant but I felt very upset about it. He wasn't offering to cut back any guests from his family, yet for some reason I had to. I'd never seen this side of him before. I went for a chat with my mum and told her my doubts but she persuaded me it was far too late in the day to change my mind and that I was just getting 'cold feet', as most brides did at some stage.

In my head, the words started repeating over and over, like a mantra: 'Don't marry him. Don't marry him.'

About ten days before the wedding, I was lying on my bed trying to picture myself walking down the aisle in my wedding dress, and I just couldn't see it. My dress looked black rather than white and there were dead leaves all over the floor of the church, blowing in the wind. In despair, I asked 'If there are any angels out there, please tell me what to do.'

And there was the voice in my head again, saying 'Don't marry him, don't marry him.' And I realised that that voice had been an angel all along.

When I told him I was calling off the wedding, he got really nasty. 'Good,' he said, 'because I don't want to marry you either.' We'd bought a house together but he changed the locks so I couldn't get in any more, then he started telling all our friends that I was frigid and all sorts of horrible things. How could I ever have thought I was in love with this man?

I had booked the honeymoon and still had the tickets, so I decided to go by myself just to have a rest and recuperate from the stress of the last few weeks. While I was there, I went for a walk and sat down on a wall at the edge of the beach. Suddenly a ball bounced against the wall beside me and a man came running after it. When he saw me he stopped and asked if I was OK. I ended up telling him about breaking off my engagement and he seemed to understand exactly why I had done it. We went for a cup of coffee – and the upshot is that eighteen months later, I was married to him. He is a kind man who genuinely loves me and we've been happy together ever since.

I don't know anyone who has ever made a decision like Grace's after repeated warnings from angels and lived to regret it. If it's not meant to be, it's not meant to be. The angels know best!

Message at the Altar

If you think Grace called off her wedding at short notice, wait till you hear about Sheila!

I was standing at the altar with my fiancé by my side, listening intently to the vicar who was marrying us. When it got to the part when he said 'Do you, Sheila James, take this man, Raymond Parks, to be your lawful wedded husband?' I opened my mouth and heard the words 'No, never. No!' come out. The voice was loud and clear, but it wasn't mine. My fiancé looked stunned, the guests started muttering behind us and I burst into tears.

The vicar led us to a side room to talk and, through clenched teeth, my fiancé told me we had to get back out there and complete the ceremony because I was making him look a fool. He told me that everything had been paid for – the reception, the honeymoon, the flowers, the clothes – and it wouldn't be refundable. Not once did he say that he loved me.

Even though I was embarrassed by the words that had come out of my mouth at the altar, I knew I would be making a big mistake if I married him. 'I'm sorry,' I said, 'but I can't go through with it. We're really not suited to each other.'

Instantly his attitude changed. 'In that case, I'm going to sue you for all the expenses incurred. You can pay for the whole thing. And you can give me damages for the embarrassment caused as well.'

That's when I knew for sure I was well out of it. My fiancé was a very controlling person who bullied me and made me feel stupid a lot of the time. I don't think I would have had the courage to say 'no' myself but I am so grateful to the angel who put the words into my mouth. It saved me a great deal of unhappiness in the future.

That evening, I went for dinner with my mother and father, and my dad ordered a bottle of champagne.

'What's that for?' I asked.

'We're celebrating that you didn't marry that man,' he said. 'Your mum and I always thought he was wrong but we couldn't tell you before now.'

Thank goodness my angel did!

It's always strange hearing a different voice coming out of your mouth. When it happens to me during a reading, the voice has a different intonation to mine, and it tends to use more precise, better English than I do. I've never started speaking in a foreign language – not yet, anyway – but I've come out with some big words I would never normally use, and it never fails to surprise me.

The Wrong Business Partner

We all make mistakes. I've made my fair share over the years. You can always get back onto the right path but it's not necessarily easy. Sometimes challenges are sent to make us learn a lesson. That was probably the case with me and the catering business, as it was with a woman called Susie, who had her own very successful interior design business.

My business had been running for almost four years and it was going from strength to strength. All my work came through personal recommendations, and every client for whom I designed a room or a whole house seemed to be delighted with the results. After a while, as the business got bigger, I found I was getting bogged down in administrative issues, such as invoicing and VAT, that were taking me away from the creative side of things, so I decided to bring in a financial director to help out. I came across someone who seemed very knowledgeable and who had lots of ideas for saving me money, so I agreed to take him on. I was very busy at the time and he seemed like the answer to my prayers. Looking back, there was a little warning voice in my head but I dismissed it because I needed help so badly.

Seven months down the line, when I walked into the office one day I heard a voice in my head saying 'Theft!' At first I dismissed it but four times that week I heard the word 'Theft', and then 'Theft – your loss!' I decided I would have to keep my eyes open to find out what it all meant.

At the end of the week, my financial director came to me and said we needed to apply for a bank loan to see us through a cash crisis.

'What's the problem?' I asked, surprised. 'I've been working flat out. We shouldn't have a cash crisis.'

But he insisted that we did.

'I'll have to look at the books to see what's going on,' I told him.

'Don't you trust me?' he complained. 'I'm supposed to be in charge of the books, not you.'

But I insisted. 'If I'm going to the bank to ask for money, I need to have a clear picture of what problems the business has,' I told him.

I went through the books with a fine-tooth comb and was surprised to find that £9,000 had been taken out in cash over the last couple of months.

'What was this for?' I asked.

'I didn't take it out,' he snapped. 'It must have been you.'

But I knew I hadn't taken out that money and he was the only other person with access to the account. We got into a huge argument about it and in the end I asked him to leave the company. He said that if I wanted him to leave, I would have to give him a pay-off or he would sue me for unfair dismissal. I asked him if he wanted me to contact the police and get them to investigate the loss of the £9,000 and he went quietly after that.

I may have lost that money, but I had learned a lesson – to take my time when appointing people to look after my money. I interviewed several new candidates for the job and while I was talking to one of them the words 'Good person, good person' were running through my head. So that's who I hired – and I was proved right.

When I met Susie I got a sense straight away that she had been conceived as a twin but that her sibling had died in the womb, very early on in the pregnancy. This is commoner than you might think and when it happens, the twin that has passed over often acts as a spirit guide for the one who is born alive. People to whom this has happened often feel isolated in the world, and they are prone to feeling guilty, as if everything is their fault. They are frequently workaholics, as Susie is, and very driven to achieve their goals.

When I told Susie that she had been a twin, she was amazed at first, but once she accepted what had happened she was able to let her twin help her with her life decisions. She gave her a name – Phoebe – and talks to her, asking her advice when she is confronting a problem.

Phoebe also helps Susie when she is working. All creativity is a form of spirituality. Without exception, everyone who writes, paints, sculpts, draws, designs, makes music or films is being guided and led by angels. They sit down and inspiration flows through them as spirits use their hands or voices as a tool with which they can help others. Many artists have tried over the centuries to describe the feeling when 'the muse' takes over, and some have said it feels as though they are being used as a vessel by something outside themselves that ideas are being channelled through. They are absolutely right. This is exactly how it works.

When writers get writers' block, or painters can't get their picture to work, or composers can't find the right chord in a sonata, it's because they are not being fully open to the help of their angels. But when they do listen and accept help, their work will flow beautifully and smoothly, as they work together in partnership with the angels.

Writing a Very Special Book

Edward, a professor of English literature, was diagnosed with a particularly nasty kind of cancer that appeared first as a tumour in his thigh muscle and spread quickly. Doctors amputated both of his legs, and gave him chemotherapy and radiotherapy but to no avail. Finally, the oncologist told him there was nothing more they could do and that he had only around six weeks to live. He came to me because he had started questioning what would happen after his death and I was able to explain that process to him, but I also got an urgent message from the spirits that he needed to put things right with his son so that they understood each other before he left the earth. Here's his story.

After the prognosis, I sat back and took stock of my life, and as part of that I went to talk to Dorothy. I knew before she told me that my only piece of unfinished business concerned my relationship with my son Graham. I love him dearly but our relationship had become very distant, which was entirely my own fault. I've always had a problem with expressing my emotions, and have been critical too many times, driving my son away. I desperately wanted to break through the impasse before I died and let Graham know how much I love him, but somehow the words just wouldn't come. For too long, I'd been out of the habit of saying 'I love you' – even to my beloved wife. Graham visited me during the cancer treatment and brought me magazines and grapes, and we'd chat politely about politics and current affairs, but I could never find a way to have the emotional conversation I really wanted to have.

Then Dorothy heard my father's voice, speaking very clearly and succinctly: 'Write a book about your life,' it said. Straight away, I thought: 'Hmm. That's not a bad idea.' I've had some interesting experiences over the years. I'd been a prisoner of war, been friends with many top authors and had served on several government sub-committees concerning the arts. All these things would be in there but, more importantly, I would be able to write about the day my son was born and I first held him in my arms, and how proud I am of what Graham has achieved in his life. It would be a lasting testament to my love.

But did I have enough time to do it justice? Would it be possible to write a book in six weeks? I got started straight away, dictating into a tape recorder from the sofa in my living room and paying a kind neighbour to type it up for me every night. Once I started, the words just flowed as if from nowhere. Sentences would come out of my mouth that I couldn't remember thinking about first, as if they came from somewhere outside myself. I'd heard some author friends talking about this process but had never experienced it myself before and it was very strange. It was the most profound thing I'd ever done, and my thoughts just flowed naturally.

I dictated every day for as long as I could before exhaustion took over, and the pages began to pile up. But the sixth week was approaching and I wasn't even half-way through my story. I dreaded dying before I'd had a chance to finish so I worked even harder. Then the sixth week passed and the seventh and the eighth, and it was as if working on the book was giving me the strength to continue living. What's more, I was taking less of my pain medication, because I didn't want to be too drowsy to write, and yet the pain wasn't bothering me. I hardly noticed it any more.

I kept writing, the months went by, and the doctors professed themselves astonished that I was still alive. By all their medical knowledge, I should have been dead long before but somehow I kept going, still writing almost every day. When I reached the last sentence, it was almost a year after I'd been told I had only six weeks to live. I wrote the final words, and then my father's voice was in my head: 'Now you are complete. Time to come home.'

I gave the finished book to Graham and waited anxiously for his opinion. A week later he came to visit me and just walked into the room and gave me a big hug. 'I love you, Dad,' he said and I told him 'I love you too.' It was a beautiful moment.

The last time I saw Edward, I knew he had only a couple of days to go but that his mission was complete. After he died I received a very beautiful letter from his wife thanking me for what I had done in urging him to write the book. She said they had kept all the tapes as well as the transcribed pages and they had been an enormous help to her as well as her son. Edward was quite a closed man and she hadn't always known what was going on inside his head, but in the book he expresses his deepest feelings.

Doctors have never been able to explain why Edward continued to live for so long after he should have been dead, but I know that angels kept him in a protective bubble while the words poured out. It was important that he learned to express his emotions during that lifetime. It was the lesson he was supposed to learn, and he did it just in the nick of time.

Where to Live

Angels can help with the big issues, such as expressing your creativity, finding love, and choosing the best career to suit your talents, but they can also help with smaller everyday matters as well. Think about how you choose a new house or flat. Whether you are buying or renting, this is one area in which everyone gets advice from angels, whether they realise it or not.

When an estate agent takes us to a new property, all our senses are alert and open. What can you smell as soon as the front door opens? Does it feel cold? How much natural light is there? What can you hear? Is there traffic noise from the main road nearby? You might stroke the wooden banister, tap the wall, turn on a kitchen tap to see what the water pressure is like. All the time you are getting messages in your head, and you use these to make your judgment: would you be happy living there or not?

Most of us make the decision very quickly. It either feels right or it doesn't and you can't always put your finger on why. That's because angels are guiding you, telling you whether it is part of your life's path to live there or not. If they're warning you against it, you will feel very uncomfortable, and may even get goose bumps.

My husband Michael has always let me be the one to choose where we live. When we found our current house, it had only just come onto the agent's books and we didn't have any particulars but the minute we got to the top of the driveway, I said to him 'This is it!'

'For goodness sake, we haven't seen the place yet,' he replied – but I just knew. We opened the door and walked in and I thought 'Yes, this is my kitchen, this is my sitting room.' I could see where all my furniture would go.

Before I start house-hunting, I always ask the angels for help. I need a place that's right for Michael and me to live in, for the family to visit, and for my animals as well (we had two dogs and two cats the last time I moved). They've never let me down yet, although sometimes the advice only comes through at the eleventh hour.

Once I was told that the number five would be important. We searched and searched for a house that was number five but couldn't find one. The estate agents were used to all kinds of odd requests but I know they thought I was round the twist when I asked them to look out for a number five. Then one day I was talking to a friend about our problems and he said that he was selling his father's house. The old man was blind and getting very frail so he was moving in with them. Michael and I went to see the house and it was perfect – just the right situation and a lovely layout. We agreed a good and fair price. We had only known the house by its name and it wasn't until the paperwork came through that we realised it actually was a number five in the road. At least I knew I'd definitely made the right decision.

On another occasion, when I was looking for a property to rent, I was told that an owl would be significant. We found a lovely place very quickly and agreed with the agent on the spot that we would take it. It was only when we were leaving that I turned back for a final look, and saw that on the roof of the garage there was a stone owl.

It may take a while but I recommend you keep looking until you find a property you feel good about. If you are forced to stay in one that doesn't feel right – maybe because you are in too much of a hurry to get a roof over your head – there's a little ceremony you can try to cleanse any negative energy from the place. Light two white candles and a pink one and let them burn down. (Keep an eye on them so you don't burn the house down at the same time!) Say something like: 'I bring love and peace into this place [name it, if you like]. All negativity is banished from here, in the name of God and Christ and all that is good.' Do it with your heart and mean it, and this mini-exorcism will work for you.

Taking the Quickest Route

On a day-to-day level, angels can give advice on practical matters such as which outfit to wear, what meal to cook for a particular occasion, and even how to avoid traffic hold-ups when you are on your way to an important meeting! A woman called Hilary told me the following story:

When my grandmother died, I wasn't particularly bothered about the way the money and property had been split up in her will, but I was keen to have some personal objects to remember her by – maybe a piece of jewellery or a painting. She was a much-loved woman and we were all saddened by her death, rather than thinking about what we could get out of it. But a cousin who hadn't had much contact with Grandma for the last ten years called me up and told me he was contesting the will because he felt he was entitled to a much bigger share of her money than he had been given.

I called my siblings and we agreed, wearily, that we would all meet to talk about it face to face rather than arguing through lawyers and running up huge legal bills.

On the day of the meeting, I set out to drive to the place we had chosen but about halfway there, I saw a huge sign saying 'Flood warning!' and then another, with an arrow, saying 'Diversion'. I didn't give it much thought because there had been a lot of rain recently and it sounded plausible. I took the diversion and arrived at the house to find my siblings were there already, but there was no sign of my cousin.

While we waited, we talked through the terms of the will and agreed that while things had to be settled the way Grandma wanted them, perhaps we could offer a couple of concessions to make our cousin feel more fairly done by. The discussion was calm and loving, without any of the heightened emotion there would have been if our cousin was present, and we agreed on a generous gesture that we hoped would satisfy him when he arrived.

He was about an hour late when he got there, complaining that he had got stuck in a flood and had had to turn and go back the way he had come and make a huge detour.

'Didn't you see the flood diversion signs?' I asked, and described to him where I had seen them.

He had passed exactly the same spot in the road and swore there had been no flood warning signs there. Could they have been removed immediately after I passed by? Why would anyone have done that? Certainly, when I drove home I checked and they were no longer there.

And then the thought came into my head that Grandma had somehow made me see a diversion sign so that we could all get together and talk without my cousin being present, and thus come up with the solution to the problem.

Hilary didn't hear her grandmother's voice that day, but she says she just had a strong sense that her grandmother arranged the flood diversion signs, and I believe that must have been the case. Anyway, the story has a happy ending because her cousin accepted their offer and all worked out well.

The View in Reading Station

Here is a salutary tale about a woman called Joanna, explaining why she will always listen to voices in her head in future.

I was on an almost empty train heading to Reading station to meet my friend Jane, as the two of us were flying off for a holiday in Egypt together. Just before the train arrived, I made a quick trip to the loo and I remember on the way back to my seat I heard a voice in my head. I thought the words it was saying were 'Skirt down', but I immediately dismissed it, my head full of travel arrangements and anticipation of our holiday.

I got off the train and walked across the station to the place where Jane and I had agreed to meet, and once again I heard the voice saying 'Skirt down', but once again I ignored it. It was only when I sat down on a metal seat that I realised what it was on about. I leapt up again straight away, feeling the cold metal on the back of my thighs. My skirt was tucked into the back of my knickers and I had walked right across the station displaying to all and sundry my knee-high travel socks and my big comfy travelling pants. I couldn't have been more embarrassed. Jane arrived soon afterwards and she fell about laughing when I told her.

Thinking back, Joanna told me she thought the voice belonged to her little brother, who had died when he was small. She was very touched that he had tried to spare her blushes, and annoyed with herself that she hadn't listened. I bet she will next time!

Car Boot Sale

Angels can help when we lose things. If you stand still and ask them, you may well find that the location of the missing items will come into your head. Rosemary was grateful for angelic intervention at a car boot sale one Saturday.

I stopped at one stall that had a pretty set of drinking glasses on display and decided to buy them for when my grandchildren come to visit. As I paid for them, I got chatting to the lady stallholder, who told me that she had made her own small business running stalls at car boot sales since her husband's death four years ago.

I moved on to another stall and was browsing there when I heard a voice in my head saying 'Purse, purse, go back.' I checked my handbag and, sure enough, my purse was missing, so I hurried back to the last stall. There were lots of people around it by this stage and I was worried that I might have put it down while chatting to the stallholder and someone had picked it up and stolen it. I looked all round the stall and there was no sign of my purse, which was extremely upsetting as I'd had around £100 cash and a bank card in there.

At that point I heard the voice in my head again, and I recognised it as belonging to my dead son Martin. 'Look under stall, under basket,' it said. I lifted a basket underneath the stall and there was my purse, with the contents intact. It must have fallen to the ground and someone had accidentally kicked it.

The stallholder invited me to sit down and share a flask of coffee with her, and I told her about hearing Martin's voice. I would never have found the purse without his help, and I'd like to take this opportunity to say a public thank you to him. I know he is with me and looking out for me every day, and I'm so grateful to him.

Life-saving Instruction

Here is another story involving an angel giving very practical guidance when it was most needed, told to me by a client called Christina.

I was driving to visit a friend one afternoon along beautiful country roads. The sun was shining and pretty-coloured wildflowers bloomed in the hedgerows. Suddenly I heard the word 'Wait!' in my head and it sounded urgent so I decided to stop. I pulled over and got out of the car to look around but couldn't see anything unusual. I was about to get back into the car when once again I heard 'Wait!' I stood around for a few minutes feeling foolish then decided to head on my way. I'd just turned the ignition key when all of a sudden a car shot around the bend up ahead and careered into a deep ditch. There was a loud crunching of metal and then silence and I could see a trail of smoke coming out of the bonnet.

I hurried up the road to find that the man inside the car was unconscious and he appeared to be trapped by the way his side door was crushed inwards. I took my mobile out of my handbag and dialled 999, describing exactly where we were, and they promised an ambulance would be there as soon as possible. After making the call, though, I realised there was a strong smell of petrol. I had to get the man out of the car before it caught fire – but how?

I spoke to the angels. 'You brought me here,' I said, 'so show me what I'm supposed to do now.'

As soon as I had spoken, there was a loud creaking sound and the back of the car slid down a bit further into the ditch. I looked closely and realised the back door had sprung open. I crawled inside the car, and the driver moaned and started to regain consciousness.

'Where am I?' he mumbled.

'You've had a car accident and I've got to get you out of the car,' I told him. In my head I asked the angels again, 'Please show me what to do.'

The idea came to me at that moment that I could press the lever to recline his seat right back, so that's what I did and I realised from that angle, I would be able to pull him out of the car through the back door. I'm not a particularly strong person, but once I got my hands under his shoulders and pulled, he slid easily out onto the grass outside.

'Get further away,' said a voice in my head, and I urged the man to stand up, leaning on my shoulder, and limp to a grassy bank about twenty feet away. I had just helped him to sit down there when flames started to lick up the outside of the car and there was a loud explosion as the fuel tank blew up.

'Oh my god, you saved my life!' he exclaimed. 'How can I ever thank you?'

I told him that a voice had told me to wait and that he must have a guardian angel watching over him, and he was very moved. Now, whenever I am setting off on a journey, I always ask my guardian angel to take care of me along the way.

If ever you find yourself in a similar emergency, try not to panic. If you spring into action without allowing space for the angels to communicate with you, you could end up doing more harm than good. But if you can be still and ask for help, the answer will be given to you, and you'll know what to do.

Plastic Surgery

Sometimes when we wake up in the morning, we feel agitated or disturbed by a dream. Whenever this is the case, it's important to analyse it and work out what upset us. It's not always straightforward because dreams can be like a mirror reflection, with what is on the right appearing to be on the left and vice versa. Start with the way the dream made you feel and work backwards from there, thinking about it logically.

What might any symbols mean? For example, if you dreamed there was a rat in your house, rather than taking it literally and calling the council's pest control department, think about what the word 'rat' means to you. Could it mean that someone is betraying you? Is someone going behind your back to 'rat' on you? Think about the underlying feeling of the dream rather than what actually happened in it.

If a loved one comes into a dream and tells you something, pay close attention. It is their way of getting a message across to you, especially if you are not listening during your waking hours. A lady I know called Matilda was about to undergo plastic surgery to change her figure – breast enhancements, tummy tucks and so forth – and two weeks before the first operation she had the following dream.

My mother was making me look in a mirror at my naked body and she said 'Look at this! Do you need this?' And when I looked I saw all the scars that would be caused by the operation. One scar on my breast had a climbing plant growing out of it. I grabbed hold of the plant to try and pull it out but the roots were too deep and it wouldn't come. Mum kept saying 'Look at the root! Look at the root!'

The next morning I felt very disturbed by the dream, which to me had definitely indicated a problem. I hadn't dreamed about Mum very often since she had died five years earlier so I was sure it must be significant in some way. I decided to go and have a private mammogram just to see if there was any substance to the feeling in the dream. Sure enough, the mammogram indicated that there was a tumour there, which turned out to be cancerous. I had to have a mastectomy, followed by breast reconstruction and I asked them to put in an enhancement and increase the other side to match. I then had to have chemo and radiotherapy and fortunately these got rid of the cancer.

After all that hospital treatment I decided not to have the tummy tuck I'd been planning. I will never put myself through any unnecessary operations again. Instead I am going to exercise like mad to get rid of that extra roll of flab round my middle. Sit-ups, here I come!

If Matilda hadn't paid heed to her dream and had gone in for the original breast enhancement operation, they would probably have found the tumour but it would have needed a second operation with a different kind of surgeon to deal with it. Her mother knew this and was trying to protect her, and a dream was the only way she could get through.

Rescue in the Park

A policeman called Jon, who is a very spiritual man, told me about his angelic intervention one day when he was out on patrol.

I'd been out on the streets for about an hour and was just walking past the park when I got a strange sense of something that wasn't good. I've thought about that feeling many times since and I can't describe it very clearly but I just felt that something was amiss, and my head was being turned towards an area of the park that is overgrown with bushes and shrubbery.

I was wary because I was out on my own that day, but then a voice said 'Help her. Go now.' It was as clear as my own voice and seemed to be coming from just beside me, but there was no one there. I walked towards the shrubbery and the voice spoke again. 'Out the back. Go now. Quickly.'

I walked round the back and, sticking out from the bushes, I saw a bare foot. I pushed back the branches and there was the body of a young girl, looking barely alive. 'Jesus!' I exclaimed out loud. I took my jacket off to cover her and then shouted at the top of my voice for help. (This was back in the days before mobiles and I didn't even have a radio.) A man walking his dog hurried over and I instructed him to go and call the emergency services, then I got down on my hands and knees to give the girl mouth-to-mouth resuscitation and chest compressions.

That young girl survived the brutal attack on her and was able to name her attacker, who was soon behind bars. She told me that as she lay there, semi-conscious, an angel came to her and told her she would be all right, so she knew she wouldn't die.

My colleagues were amazed I had found her in such thick undergrowth, and I felt I couldn't tell them about the voice, but I have heard it throughout my career. When I interview people who say that a voice told them to do something, I always know when they are genuine and when they are psychotic because I'm used to hearing voices myself.

People such as Peter Sutcliffe, the Yorkshire Ripper, who claim that voices in their heads told them to commit murder, are not listening to angels. People with psychosis are no longer in contact with reality and their brain plays tricks on them, due to brain injury or a chemical imbalance. They say that angels make them do things, but the truth is that real angels can't interfere with our free will. We *choose* what to do and the voices we hear just give us warnings or advice, while psychotic people are *made* to do whatever they do by their voices. As a police officer, Jon needs to be very clear about the distinction.

My Work with the Police

My work is not just about comforting the bereaved and passing on messages to loved ones. It can have very practical applications, such as in the work I do for the police in the UK and for the FBI in the States. I'm not allowed to write much about this, because I work with some very prominent, high-ranking people who would be embarrassed if it came out that they use a medium, but the point is that the principles are the same as for all the other life advice I've been describing in this chapter. I open myself up and ask the angels a question and keep very still as I listen for the answer.

The first case I worked on was terribly distressing, and came to me in a roundabout way a long time ago. A client of mine was a solicitor who was married to a policeman, and during a reading an image came into my head of a little girl's body. The odd thing is I remember looking up and there was a grating above my head and I was the child, which was the first time this had ever happened to me during a reading. I was communicating with this child but at the same time I could see everything she could see. She showed me the dress she was wearing and then she showed me how she had died.

I described it to the solicitor just the way I saw it, hoping it would have meaning for her, and I soon noticed she was looking at me very oddly. She asked if I knew the child's name and I told her the name that came into my head.

'Don't you listen to the news?' she asked. 'That's the little girl who's missing. There are police hunting for her everywhere.'

Through the information I gave, the police were able to find her body and in the end they apprehended her murderer. I was very shocked at the time, and uncertain when, a few months later, the police approached me and asked if I would be interested in looking at a few cold cases for them. Eventually I agreed because I believe it is my duty to use my powers to help others. If I can help the parents of a missing person to find some peace, then that is a worthwhile use of my gift.

Through a lawyer who came to one of my seminars in New York, I was contacted by the FBI and asked if I could work on some of their missing persons cases. Usually they'll just give me a couple of facts about a case – a first name, an occupation, the colour of clothing they were wearing when they went missing. Once or twice I have met a family member of the missing person, and that can be very distressing.

On one occasion I was introduced to a young man whose girlfriend had gone missing over a year earlier, and I got a cold, nasty feeling straight away. All I could see was pieces of a body – an arm, a foot, the back of a head – and I knew that the man sitting opposite me had killed her. I looked into his eyes and I think he could tell that I knew because he couldn't leave the room fast enough. I told the police what I had seen, the dismembered body was found and, after a long investigation, that man was arrested and found guilty of his girlfriend's murder.

Nowadays I do a lot of my police consultations by phone. They ring with a few details and ask me if I can give them a lead. Sometimes I can and sometimes I can't. I'll just sit with the information and see what comes to me.

The gift I have is hereditary, mainly from my mother's side of the family, although my father's mother had Romany blood. The Romanies are good, honest people with strong spiritual powers, so perhaps some of my gift comes from that part of the family as well.

Everyone has psychic abilities but not many people recognise them or choose to use them the way I do. However, everyone can make wise decisions in their own lives by listening to angels, and I strongly recommend that we all do that every single day.

Chapter 5

Psychic Children

The memory of every lifetime you've ever had is still inside you, and each period between lives is there as well, so everything that has happened to your soul is stored, as if on a computer hard drive that can't ever be wiped. Between lives, you can go back and remember what you've done and be aware of the interactions between different people you've been involved with during your lifetimes.

People are often reincarnated into the same family if they still have issues that are unresolved from last time, but the relationship between them might change – from mother and son to husband and wife, or to siblings. You might be male in one life and female in the next, depending on the lessons you need to learn. Sometimes I help clients by going into a past-life for them if I feel there is something that is preventing them from moving forwards in their current life. An understanding of the issues they were stuck on before can sometimes be the trigger they need to make changes.

Most of us forget about our past lives as we concentrate on this one, although we might occasionally get a strong sense of *déjà vu* when something triggers a distant memory. All the meaningful events are still there, though, and that's why I can help people to retrieve them through hypnotism.

Babies are born with a soul memory of their previous lives and the time when they were between lives, and this only fades gradually over the first couple of years, as they learn language and their brains become occupied with picking up the skills they need to thrive in the world. They can often see spirits that the adults around them aren't aware of, and they treat them quite naturally, finding nothing unusual in a kindly presence in the corner of the room as they drift off to sleep. In fact, it can be very comforting, as the five spirit visitors were for me when I lay in my cot as a child.

I've heard several stories of babies waving and smiling at someone who is invisible to the adults present, and usually their parents are baffled by it. I explain to them that almost always this will be a relative who has passed over and has come back to keep an eye on the new child. They tend to come at the quiet moments: while the baby is lying in his or her cot, or playing calmly on the floor, or lying peacefully in his mother or father's arms.

I've come across some children who keep their soul memory later than others and possibly never lose it. These children are very special and are here for a purpose, to help the adults around them to find their way. They can pass on messages from the other side and even tell stories of previous lives they have led. Children who have strong soul memories grow up to be very sensitive individuals. In this chapter, I'll share with you some of the beautiful anecdotes I have come across about children with psychic powers.

Recognising Nana

It's sad when people die too young to meet their grand-children. They can't share all the milestones of first steps, first tooth, first words, first day at school, and the funny things that children say as they learn our language. But I always explain to any clients whose parents have died before their children were born that their spirits will be keeping a very close eye on the new family members. They wouldn't miss them for anything! And what's more, the children will know them as well. Here's a story that a client called Marion told me:

My four-year-old son Alex and I were looking through a photo album together when suddenly he pointed at a picture of my mother, who had died not long before he was born.

'That's my angel nana!' he said. 'I like her.'

I had never called my mother Nana, so I questioned him about the name.

'That's what she said her name was,' he told me.

'When did she say that?'

'When she comes to see me,' he said in an impatient tone, as if surprised I didn't know about it.

I felt my skin prickle all over as I asked him more questions about these visits.

'She comes to see me when I'm playing with my toys in the bedroom, or when I'm in bed at night after you leave the room. She doesn't talk very much but she likes to watch me playing.'

'Do you know where she is now?' I asked, on the verge of tears because I felt so emotional.

He considered this for a moment. 'I'm not sure but she said she really likes it there. I asked her if I could come and visit but she said not for a very long time.'

'Why do you call her an angel?' I asked. It wasn't a word that I had ever explained to him.

'Because that's what she is,' he said, as if any fool knew that.

'Will you let me know next time she comes?' I asked.

'Maybe,' he said doubtfully. 'But it's me she comes to see. She said I'm her special boy and she loves me very much.'

It sounded exactly like something my mum would say, so that's when I knew for sure it must be her who was visiting Alex. And I was so glad, because she died while I was pregnant and I was broken-hearted at the time that she would never meet him – yet it turns out that she has. I told him he is very lucky to have an angel nana and next time she came he was to give her my love.

Over the years since then Alex has sometimes given us some very practical messages from Mum. For example, my sister had been trying to buy a house she had fallen in love with, just two doors down from where we had grown up, but the sale fell through when she was gazumped by some buyers coming in with a higher offer. She was bitterly disappointed, but Alex told me that Mum said not to give up, that she should go back and try again. When I gave the message to my sister, she decided to phone the estate agent 'just in case' and she was over the moon when she heard that the new buyers had had to pull out because they couldn't raise the money. She was back in the running again, but this time she renegotiated the price to a level she could afford and the sellers accepted.

We feel very privileged to have this special communication with Mum and to benefit from the advice she can give us – all thanks to my son Alex.

Most children will stop seeing spirits at around the time they are learning to talk, but that doesn't mean they aren't still visiting. I recommend continuing to talk about the person who has passed over, including them as a member of your family, sharing memories of them and keeping their photograph on display. They haven't gone away; they are just at a different stage of the journey than you for now.

His Father's Pen

Jonathan and Adrian are stepbrothers who have different mothers but shared the same father until he died a couple of years ago. Their mothers live close to each other, so they have grown up with a real closeness between them, despite a twelve-year age gap. Shortly after their dad's death, four-year-old Jonathan came to sixteen-year-old Adrian with a very strange message:

Jonathan told me that Father wanted me to have something of his and that I would find it at the back of the little drawer at the top of his writing desk.

'How do you know?' I asked.

'He came and told me in the night,' Jonathan replied.

Just to humour him, I went to look in the back of the drawer in the writing desk, and there I found my father's special fountain pen. Mum had given it to him for his fortieth birthday and I had always begged him to let me use it because it made my handwriting look fantastic. I even remembered him saying to me, 'One day it will be yours.'

I was overjoyed to have that pen, but curious about the communication Jonathan was having with our father. Several times after that he came to me with messages about all kinds of things: the subjects I was studying at school, a bully that was being mean to me, even a cricket match I was due to play in. These weren't things that four-year-old Jonathan could have known anything about yet his advice always made perfect sense. Could he really be communicating with our father's spirit? I became more and more convinced he must be.

One day, I was planning to go horse riding, which was one of my favourite hobbies.

'Father says don't go today or you'll have an accident,' Jonathan told me very seriously.

'But I'm all ready. I was just heading off.'

'Father doesn't want you to go today,' he said.

I cancelled my plans, and from then on I always asked Jonathan if it was safe before I went off for a day's riding.

Most of the time he would say it was, and sometimes he'd tell me it wasn't. I've got no way of knowing if I would have had an accident if I went on a day he told me wasn't safe. But I would rather not take the chance.

I think Adrian is very wise. It seems as though Jonathan is lucky enough to have a direct communication with his father and I hope he keeps it as he grows up. They both understand that their father is there to help them, and that is a great comfort for growing boys.

A Gifted Little Girl

Some friends of mine are the grandparents of a quite extraordinary little girl called Ellie. The first time we met she couldn't stop staring at me, and I realised straight away that it was because she is psychic herself and the spirits were telling her about me. She and I communicate very directly and honestly about her gift, although she is still only six years old. I think it's important that she understands not everyone can do what she does, but that she learns never to be afraid of the spirits who visit her, and how to use the information they bring to do good.

Her relatives found it a bit spooky when she first started talking about spirit world, when she was very young. Here's what her mother told me:

Ellie's Aunt Claire was sitting with Ellie on her lap as she looked through some photographs she'd taken at the Lord Mayor's Show in London. One picture showed a horse and carriage travelling in the ceremonial parade and Ellie, who was only two and a half, blurted out: 'Horse and carriage. I died there.'

She didn't seem at all upset, but it was such an odd thing to say that Claire reported it back to me. How did she know these words? Did she have any idea what death was?

Shortly afterwards I was sitting at my computer looking through old photos of London when a picture of a Duke of Wellington statue came up. Ellie suddenly became agitated.

'That's where I died, Mummy,' she said. 'Don't you remember?'

I questioned her carefully, in terms I thought she would understand, but what she was telling me very clearly was that she had died in a past life at the age of seven when she was knocked over by a horse and carriage.

'You were my mummy then as well,' she said, 'but you had dark hair.'

She even mentioned the street in London where she had lived. I looked it up and, sure enough, there is still a street with that name, just near London Bridge. How could she have known that at the age of two unless it was as she said?

'What was your name in that life?' I asked.

'Elinor,' she said firmly. 'Not Ellie.'

My husband and I did some research and found out that the Duke of Wellington statue Ellie had reacted to had been moved to Aldershot in 1885 and it has recently been restored there, so one day we took her to see it. She became very quiet and thoughtful, and confirmed that it was right in front of that statue that she had been run over and killed. It was a most peculiar moment for all of us.

That's not the only past life that Ellie can remember. When she was four, she came to me one day and told me that she once had another mummy who left her on a doorstep. After that, she had been given the chance to be happy this time round and had chosen my husband and I as her mummy and daddy.

It never ceases to amaze me, the things that Ellie comes out with. It's as natural to her as breathing. She just tells me her observations, without any other motive except to explain it to me so that I understand.

When she was six she came running into the kitchen in huge excitement telling me she had just seen an angel in the hall.

'What did he look like?' I asked.

'He had brown shoes with buttons up to there.' She pointed to her anklebone. 'Then skin.' She pointed to her shin. 'And short trousers with a blue shirt that wasn't tucked in.'

I was amazed at the detail of the description and expected her to be too over-excited to get to sleep that night, but in fact she slept like a log. It didn't bother her at all. She seems to be quite relaxed about visits from spirits.

Ellie has an invisible friend who she calls Sala, and it's quite a volatile relationship. Sometimes they fall out, and then not long after they are best friends again, so it can be hard to keep up. Ellie insists on Sala being involved in all aspects of family life, and I'm always conscious that I must look a bit strange when I'm doing things like lifting her imaginary friend into a supermarket trolley, but no one has said anything to me yet.

As a family, we suffered a terrible tragedy when Ellie's older brother Ryan died at the age of seventeen, but Ellie is still able to talk to him and bring me messages from him and that is an incredible comfort. To know that he is still with us brings me peace of mind.

My husband never used to believe in the afterlife, and at first he thought Ellie's pronouncements were just a child's fantasy world. But she comes out with so many provable statements that he has changed his mind now. At her age there is no way she could possibly know all the things she tells us. There's no question that she is in touch with spirits.

Personally, I can't wait to see what happens to Ellie as she grows older. She already has such a wise head on young shoulders that I have a feeling she will do a lot of good in the world, and I intend to give her as much guidance as I can when I am around her. She is a very special little girl.

The Little Blind Angel

When their son Ben was born blind, Roger and Sarah were at first grief-stricken for all the experiences they thought he would never be able to enjoy and the problems his life would bring. But it wasn't long before they realised that he had been given massive gifts to compensate for his lack of sight.

Ben learned to speak very early, with a clear, un-babylike tone, and he also had a beautiful singing voice from the age of two.

I think he was only three when he said to us both one day: 'You need to know that I have come to help you. I know a lot more than you do and I need you to listen to me.'

We both laughed at first to be told this by a toddler, but there was something about the seriousness of his tone that stopped me. 'It's true,' a little voice in my head told me and I got goose bumps down my arms.

Then, when he was just four, Ben sat down at the piano one day. At first he just banged on the notes as any four-year-old child would, but before long he could pick out tunes and within a week he could play any music he heard by ear. If he liked something he heard on the radio or TV, he would sit down and play it, no matter how difficult it was. That's when Roger and I first knew we had a gifted child, but at that stage we had no idea quite how gifted he was.

Ben was a very happy child and didn't have an aggressive bone in his body. If his brother and sister were fighting, he'd stand between them and make them stop and think about what they were doing until they backed down and calm prevailed again. Everyone who met him said he was a little angel.

'How did you know that?' he asked a friend of mine when she said it, leaving her startled. 'How did you know I was an angel?'

I think he had known he was an angel since the day he was born but it took me a while longer to be convinced.

One day when he was six, Ben said something that really shocked me at the time. 'I'm not going to have a long life, Mummy, but it will be a very happy one.'

'What do you mean? No one knows how long their life will be.'

'I do,' he said, and for some reason I believed him, but it made me too sad to think about it so I put it out of my head.

Ben started warning us about things, and without thinking I always took his advice. If he said 'Don't drive the car today, Mummy', I would let Roger do the driving. He always sat between his brother and sister in the back seat on family outings, and several times he warned us that there was a queue ahead, or another driver overtaking, so that you would tend to forget he was blind. He had better road sense than we did!

One day when we were up north, he said, 'Daddy, be careful, there's a tractor coming.'

'OK,' Roger said, and slowed the car.

A minute later, we rounded a bend and came upon a tractor laden with bales of hay taking up most of the width of the lane. Roger had to pull right over into the hedgerow to avoid it. There was no way Ben could have heard it from so far back. He just knew it was there.

I began to test Ben without telling him, to find out more about his gift, and every time I tested him there was no other explanation for the things he knew except that he was telling us the truth and that he was an angel.

One night at bedtime, he said to me softly, 'You don't have to keep testing me, Mummy. I do know.'

Suddenly I felt very emotional. 'You told me your life will be short,' I said. 'Do you know how short?'

'I will tell you when my life is coming to an end,' he said. 'Don't worry, Mum. It's all going to be fine.'

Ben is still alive at the time of writing. I'm not sure what lesson he was supposed to bring for Roger and Sarah but they have become a very spiritual family. They're always laughing and sharing jokes with each other, but they know that they are honoured because they live with an angel in their midst.

Children with some form of physical handicap are usually evolved souls living their last lifetime on earth and they give an enormous amount back to their families. They are angels here on earth, bringing joy and wisdom to everyone around them.

Damaged at Birth

My daughter Tanya used to run an organisation that helped disabled children to get involved with horses and she found they loved the connection with these big, gentle animals and were able to communicate with them even if they didn't have any verbal skills at all. I understand this, because I have found that I can communicate with severely disabled children at a psychic level, just as I can with animals (more on that in the next chapter).

I first realised I could do this when a client called Wendy came to see me for a reading. She had a little boy called Max who was damaged during childbirth so badly that he couldn't speak, walk or do anything for himself, but as soon as I met him, he started talking to me psychically. First of all he told me about some presents his mum had bought him for his birthday the following week. I passed this back to her and she was astonished.

'How on earth did you know?'

'Max told me,' I explained.

Once she got over her amazement that I could communicate with him, she had all sorts of questions she wanted to ask, so I acted as an intermediary. Among the revelations that came out, Max told me that he didn't like one of the nurses who looked after him because she was spiteful.

Wendy decided to keep a close eye on this particular nurse and a week later, when she thought no one was watching, the nurse pinched Max hard on his leg. Wendy marched into the room and sacked her on the spot. I'm glad to say they got a new nurse, who Max told me was very kind.

When he was eight, Max asked me to warn his mother that he wouldn't see his tenth birthday. He wanted her to know in advance so it didn't come as a huge shock.

'Every year we have him is a blessing,' she told me sadly as she took in the news.

And Max was right, because he died of an epileptic fit just a couple of weeks before he would have been ten. Wendy told me that the size of the payout they got from the NHS for damages was reduced because he had led such a short life. It's a strange old world, isn't it? But I know that he had a very happy time here on earth and brought a lot of joy to his parents as well.

I also used to communicate with a little boy called Noah who had been starved of oxygen at birth. He was blind and the doctors told his parents that he would never be able to sit up on his own or move around. His grandfather brought him to me to see if I could get through, and straight away he started chatting.

He told me that the doctors had got it wrong. He said he could actually see but just had problems focusing. He said he would be able to stand up and walk one day, although he would always need help getting around. He told me to tell his family that he was much stronger than they thought he was and that he wanted to be left alone to develop his muscles. If they would stop picking him up and carrying him all the time, he said he would improve faster.

I passed all this on and they were over the moon. Noah is five now, and a real little character with many more abilities than the doctors ever thought he would have. When he is brought to see me he issues instructions to his family through me and tells them what is going to happen. Recently he told his mum that she is going to have another baby next year and that this one will be fine. Every time I see him his condition has improved markedly and I know that he will bring great gifts to his family throughout his life.

All the disabled children I've met have strong soul memories and psychic capabilities. They face huge physical challenges, of course, but they are born into their families for a positive reason and can bring great joy.

A Life-Threatening Illness

Celia and Henry were devastated when their six-year-old son Jason was diagnosed with leukaemia. It's every parent's worst nightmare. They hurtled into a frantic routine of hospital visits, and Jason was treated with chemotherapy, radiotherapy and finally a bone marrow transplant before doctors finally told them that they had run out of options and that, sadly, they couldn't save Jason's life. I'll let Celia tell the story.

After the doctors told us there was nothing left to try, I fell apart. They couldn't tell us exactly how long he had to live but they hinted that it was weeks rather than months. I broke down in the car park outside and sobbed until I felt completely drained. Somehow I had to pull myself together and put on a brave face in front of Jason and our two other sons, Alastair and Geoffrey. They both knew that Jason was sick, but we hadn't mentioned the possibility that he might die.

One night just after the terminal diagnosis, Geoffrey, who is only four, came into my bedroom and woke me up.

'Mummy,' he said, 'Grandma came to see me and she said she has saved Jason. He isn't going to the angels any more. They are coming to him instead.'

My eyes were brimming with tears. His grandma – my mother – had died five years earlier. 'That's lovely, darling,' I said. 'Thank you for telling me.'

He continued: 'And she said that the drugs have done all they can and are not helping Jason any more so you should stop them now.'

It was such a grown-up sentence for a four-year-old that I sat straight upright and stared at him. 'Are you sure? Grandma really told you that?'

'Yes,' he said, before climbing into bed to snuggle up with me.

I lay awake thinking about what he'd said. Jason was still taking drugs with horrible side effects that made his face and joints all swollen and his muscles weak. If he could stop taking these, it would at least make his final weeks more comfortable. I decided I would talk to the doctors the next morning.

It was a difficult decision to make but the doctors agreed that Jason's quality of life would be better over his final weeks if they weaned him off the drugs, so that's what they did.

Within a week all the puffiness went down and he seemed to have renewed energy, getting up to play with his brothers without getting tired. I was filled with joy as I watched him laughing and running around in a way that he hadn't done for months, but then I would remember that he only had a short time to live and I'd be cast right back down again.

'Don't over-tire yourself,' I cautioned.

'But Mummy,' Jason said. 'It's OK. An angel came and told me that I could play again and that I wasn't to be frightened.'

A little germ of hope was planted in my heart, but it wasn't until we went to the hospital for a check-up exactly a month after he came off the drugs that I realised I was watching a miracle in process. I knew Jason looked much better, with a healthy skin tone, and that he had got his appetite and his energy back, but when the stunned doctors told me that his blood tests were completely normal, without a trace of the disease, I almost fainted with joy. I knew my family had truly been blessed by the angels. Jason still goes back for a check-up every few months but there has never been any recurrence of the leukaemia and he is now a normal, healthy boy.

I like the fact that the angels chose to speak to Jason's younger brother Geoffrey. At only four years old, he wouldn't have any of the rational doubts that an older person might have had. It was his grandma speaking and he just believed what she said without question. Celia and Henry's brains were too full of sorrow and anxiety for them to be able to hear any angelic messages that came through, but a child could listen without pre-judging.

Mummy's New Husband

It is not uncommon for the angels to pass messages through children. A woman I know lost her husband to cancer when she was still only forty years old. She struggled to carry on, being a single mum to their little seven-year-old daughter Anais and just getting through the days. She was a very kind, attractive woman and several men were interested in dating her but she couldn't face it because she missed her husband too much.

Eighteen months after my loss, Anais came to me one day with a message. 'Daddy talked to me last night and he told me that you should get married again.'

I was overwhelmed at first. While I had been nursing him through the cancer, he kept telling me that I should move on and find someone else after I got over the sadness at his death, but as far as I was concerned it was far too soon.

'Did you see him? How did he look?' I asked.

'He looks fine. Sort of glowing a little bit. He came and sat on the floor by my bed and chatted to me. He even told me who you should marry – his friend Ted.'

I didn't feel ready at all but I began to think about the suggestion. Ted was a good man who I hadn't seen since the funeral. I decided to give him a ring and tell him what Anais had said.

'I know this sounds weird,' I began, and then I told him the story.

'If he wants us to, I think we should meet up and have a drink,' he replied.

We started seeing each other as friends but as the months went by we seemed to be getting closer and closer. It was another year before I was sufficiently through my grief to let the relationship develop into anything beyond friendship but eventually it all happened as my first husband had suggested, and Ted and I got married. We always raise a glass of good wine in memory of my first husband on his birthday and on the day he died. I can't believe I have been so lucky as to have two such special men in my life, who are both wonderful to me.

If her husband's spirit had come to her initially with the suggestion, I'm sure she wouldn't have listened. She would have thought her brain was playing tricks, or would have dismissed the idea completely as disloyal to her husband's memory. But Anais was open enough to listen and accept, and because the message came through their daughter, my friend paid attention and let the idea be planted in her brain.

Saving Granny

A woman called Jean was bringing up her six-year-old daughter Chloe on her own, after her husband Ron died young. She had a busy life, with a job as well as a house to run, but she still kept an eye on Ron's mum, who lived a few streets away. One day she had a very alarming experience:

Chloe was sitting at the kitchen table drawing pictures as I began the preparations for supper. Suddenly, out of nowhere, she said 'Dad wants you to go and see Granny.'

'What do you mean?' I asked, puzzled.

'He just told me in my head that you have to go and see her now.'

I had seen his mum two days earlier and she'd been fine but there was something about the certainty of Chloe's tone that made me pick up the phone and dial her number. It rang and rang but there was no reply and I knew that was odd because she was never out at that time of day. She would normally have been sitting in front of the TV with her supper on her lap.

I still thought it was a false alarm, but I put Chloe in the car and drove round there, just to set my mind at rest. When we arrived, she didn't answer the door so I let myself in using my spare keys and called out her name. There was no reply. I wandered round, looking in each room, then noticed the back kitchen door was open. On the ground outside, Ron's mum was lying unconscious.

I grabbed the phone and called an ambulance then crouched down beside her. I thought I could hear her breathing faintly so I got a blanket to keep her warm and talked to her quietly until the ambulance arrived.

It turned out she had had a heart attack but she made a good recovery in hospital. The doctors told me that if she had been left out in the cold unattended she wouldn't have survived much longer. It was thanks to Chloe – and my husband – that she lived.

As we chatted to her afterwards, she said that while she was lying on the ground she had heard Ron's voice in her head saying 'Don't worry. You'll be fine. Chloe will get help.' And so she did.

Chloe was very proud of her role in the rescue and I know that the bond between her and her granny was strengthened by the events that day when they both got messages from Ron. She often talks to her now and I'm sure she'll continue to get good advice from her as she grows up – both before and after her granny's death.

Invisible Friends

Both of my own daughters are psychic. I recognised it first in Nicky, the eldest, because as a child she used to look around her as if she saw things. I would look in the same direction and sometimes I would see what she was seeing and sometimes not. Then there was the time when I had my pulmonary embolism and she announced at breakfast that she knew I was going to be OK because my mother had told her in the night. I always encouraged her to be in touch with the angels and although she doesn't work with spirit, she helps at some of my seminars. I know her so well that I can just look at her and tell when she's off and the spirits are communicating with her.

My younger daughter Tanya had an invisible friend as a child. Usually this means that the child in question was a twin in the womb and the other baby died very early on but stays around to look after their sibling. Tanya's friend was called Emma, and I treated her as a member of our family, setting a place for her at the dinner table and asking after her. Emma had a little dog called Toby and Tanya was forever saying to me 'Don't shut the door! Toby hasn't got in yet,' and I'd have to hold the door open ten seconds longer.

I've heard some parents worry that an invisible friend is the sign of a mental health problem, or that it means their child is lonely or isolated, but I don't believe this at all. I believe it's a sign of a very spiritual, creative child, and I know Emma was a great help to Tanya when she was growing up.

Tanya was bullied at her first school by a nasty bunch of girls who did things like tying her long hair to the back of the chair or grabbing her schoolbag and hiding it. She was miserable at the time, but at least she had Emma on her side. One day she was in the cloakroom on her own when Emma said firmly 'It's time to leave.' Tanya didn't even stop to tie her shoelaces. She just picked up her coat and bag and started to walk out of the room. The bullies were on their way in, but Tanya said firmly 'I'm leaving!' and pushed her way past them. Tanya believes that Emma's help saved her from being bullied that day.

I spoke to the staff at the school but wasn't happy with the way they were dealing with the problem so I finally decided to move Tanya to a new school. After her first day there, she came home calm and happy, and told me: 'When I stood in assembly this morning in my new school uniform, Emma was standing beside me in the same new uniform and I knew that everything would be fine. I'm going to like it there.'

Emma started to fade out of Tanya's life when she was in her late teens, but she would still come back in times of trouble. She shared everything with Emma and I believe it helped to make her the happy, confident person she is today.

I never questioned Tanya's friendship with Emma for a second and in fact I think I saw her myself once. We were living in a big Victorian house while I was pregnant with Tanya and one day when I was sitting having a rest in bed, a little girl with blonde curly hair came in and looked at me. She was wearing Victorian clothes – an ankle-length blue dress with a white apron tied on top, and black boots on her feet. She came up to the bed, smiled at me then disappeared. I've described her to Tanya and we think it might be the same person, although when Tanya saw Emma she was always wearing the same clothes as her – school uniform, riding gear, or whatever.

Death in the Womb

The soul enters a baby at the moment of conception, so even if you miscarry very early, at seven or eight weeks pregnant, the child is still a part of your family. They have chosen you as a parent and will stick around to look out for you. I have often found that these children move things around in the household as a way of getting your attention – maybe pieces of jewellery, papers, car keys or ornaments might move from place to place. They won't disappear completely but it might take you a while to find them.

I lost a baby, a little boy, back in my twenties, and he sometimes turns up even now. I keep a magnifying mirror in the drawer of my bedside table and no one else would have any reason to remove it from there, but one day when I went to look for it, it had gone. I asked everyone in the house but they all said they hadn't seen it. Eventually, after I had looked everywhere, I said out loud, 'Whoever it is, will you please put my mirror back in place.' And within a day, it was back there again.

I hope you find this comforting if you have lost a baby yourself. They are still around, they care about you, and they are happy.

A little girl I know called Leanne has an invisible friend called Peggy. Peggy is much older than her, like an older sister who gives advice. When I first met the family, I could see straight away that Leanne's mother had had a termination in her early twenties and that Peggy is that soul of the baby that was never born. She had picked out their family to spend this lifetime with and is continuing to do so as a guardian angel who looks after them. Leanne insists that a place is set for Peggy at the dinner table, and even that they leave space for her in the car when going off on holiday. As with Tanya and Emma, Peggy was able to reassure Leanne on her first day at school, and she helps her through all the problems she faces.

Friends for Boys Too

Invisible friends aren't just for girls. A banker I know who is now in his fifties told me about his childhood friend:

I was an only child but I was never lonely because I had my invisible friend Roger. Wherever I went, he went, and before I went to sleep I would always say goodnight to him. There was a long privet hedge at the back of my garden and we used to go up there and march up and down, or play peek-a-boo or chases with each other. The adults would say to me 'Aren't you good playing all by yourself!' and that's when I realised they couldn't see Roger. I don't see him any more now myself but I often think about him and know he is out there somewhere still helping me. If I have a problem I ask his advice, and if something goes well, I say 'Thanks for your help'.

If a child of yours has an invisible friend, I would advise you not to bombard them with questions. Let them know they can talk to you about their friend, and make room for them at the dinner table if asked, but don't make a big thing out of it. Whatever happens, they shouldn't get the idea that there is something wrong with them. You want them to stay part of the world and not feel like an oddball.

Invariably children with invisible friends will have psychic gifts as well. As with any other talents, they should be encouraged to nurture them and never ridiculed. They have a lot to give in this lifetime and we are fortunate to have them around.

Children fascinate me. They are all psychic to an extent because they are still close to their soul memory from the time between lives and their heads are less cluttered with all the minutiae of modern life. The same is true of animals, and that's what I'm going to look at in the next chapter.

Chapter 6

Psychic Animals

We've all noticed how quickly animals make up their minds about a stranger. Dogs will either go straight up to them, tails wagging, or they will stand and growl, their hackles rising. And cats are no less clear at making their feelings known, as every cat owner knows. Horses might refuse to let some people ride them while welcoming others. Even wild creatures who are unaccustomed to humans will trust some and distrust others on sight. It's common to talk about animals having a 'sixth sense' but in my view, this 'sixth sense' comes from the angels, who are whispering in their ears.

I have a blind cat called Henry and he loves people, but occasionally he will turn his back and walk away when a new person comes to the house. No matter how hard you try to win him over, if he doesn't like you, he doesn't like you. When I run a workshop, he sometimes comes in and walks round the group of roughly ten people, sussing them out. If he senses someone he doesn't like, he will literally turn his back on them and nothing they can do – not even offers of food – will tempt him back again.

I think animals have this heightened spiritual connection for the same reason as young children do: because their brains aren't cluttered up with all the information that fills our heads when we get a little bit older. They haven't had science lessons at school teaching them a rigid world view in which everything has to be explained according to the laws of physics. They don't read newspapers or watch TV programmes in which people who believe in spirits are mocked, therefore they can express their feelings in an unselfconscious way.

The bond between pet and pet owner is a very special one. If you have chosen a kitten or puppy from a litter, I'm sure you will have followed your 'instincts' (in other words, the nudges from angels) and the animal in question will probably have come rushing up to you because it is following angelic advice as well. Sometimes there is a mismatch and the relationship doesn't work out: I know someone who was most perturbed when one of her cats left home and moved in with a gay couple up the street, but I think it was probably best for both of them!

Usually the bond is a very deep one of love and, as with bonds between humans, it will survive after death.

Fetching the Newspaper

Cats and dogs become part of the family they live with. Children play with them, busy working professionals stroke them to help relieve stress, old people cuddle them on their laps, and everyone in the household knows their favourite foods, toys and places to snooze. The death of a pet who has been part of your life for ten to twenty years is a huge trauma, and particularly so for those who live alone and relied on the animal for company and comfort. There's a tendency among those who don't have pets to dismiss the very deep sorrow caused when a much-loved pet dies, but make no mistake – it is a genuine bereavement, with all the stress and grief that entails.

Like human beings, animals have many lives and periods between lives. When they pass over, they can look back and see the pain their former owners are going through, and many will return to try and bring some comfort in whatever way they can. Here are some stories I've heard about this phenomenon, beginning with an elderly man called Dick:

My dog Hannah was the most intelligent, loyal creature on the planet. She was a Labrador cross with a beautiful yellow coat and compassionate eyes that made you feel as though you could see into her soul. For ten years after the death of my wife, Hannah was my only companion and when she died, she left a huge hole in my life that I thought could never be filled again. I'm in my eighties so it didn't seem fair to get another dog, because what would happen to them when I die? And anyway, no other dog could ever compete with Hannah.

She was incredibly talented and did many things for me both in and out of the house. Every morning she would go and fetch my newspaper from the newsagent's on the corner and leave it out on the porch by the comfy chair where I liked to sit reading and watching the world go by. She could fetch a sweater for me if I got cold, pick up things I dropped on the floor and pass them back to me, and when she got hungry she would bring me her food bowl in her mouth as a hint!

After she was gone I had to start doing things for myself again, but it was a real struggle. My walking isn't very good now but if I wanted a newspaper I had to get myself ready and limp down the road with my walking stick to pick it up because our local newsagent doesn't do home deliveries. But one morning when I was feeling especially stiff and achey, I came out of the house to find my paper sitting in its usual place by the easy chair on the porch. How could that be? The idea came into my head that Hannah was somehow responsible but I couldn't explain how.

Since then, on the days when I am too creaky to get my own paper, I often find it sitting on the porch in our special place. I am convinced that Hannah is still looking after me and I often talk to her in my head to thank her.

Angels are pure energy and have all kinds of powers that are beyond our comprehension. They can move cars out of the way of accidents and lift human beings out of danger, so having a morning paper delivered is well within their capabilities, as I explained to Dick when he told me his story.

Clawing at the Bedside Table

My own cat Leo died a year ago and is still seeking my attention from beyond the grave. He was a beautiful cat, with a strong personality and used to make me laugh because he was almost human in the way he let me know what he wanted, whether it was food, stroking, or a door opened to let him out. He had different miaows for each occasion and he'd come up and nudge me with his head if I wasn't doing exactly what he wanted, when he wanted it.

If I was still asleep in bed in the morning when Leo wanted me to get up and prepare his breakfast, he would come into the bedroom and start clawing at the cloth that covered my bedside table. More than once, this resulted in my alarm clock, book and the little ornaments I keep there ending up on the floor, but no matter how much I told him off, he still used it as a way to get my attention in the morning.

Imagine my huge surprise when one morning, about six months after his death, I was woken by a clattering noise as all the things from my bedside table tumbled to the floor. The cloth was pulled askew in the same way as it used to be when Leo clawed at it. Straight away, I knew it was him, coming back to tell me he was OK. There was no other explanation.

It has happened several times since then, and it always makes me smile at all the fond memories I have of my bossy old friend.

Sitting on Her Lap

Edith was very elderly and in poor health so when her faithful Highland terrier Trixie was run over by a car, she descended into a deep depression. Her family were worried because she was hardly eating anything and it seemed as if she had stopped taking an interest in life. Then one day, she had a visitor ...

I missed Trixie so badly that, to be honest, I couldn't see any point in going on after her death. I dragged myself through the motions of getting up and dressed but I felt tired and weepy the whole time. Then, about three months after Trixie died, I went to sit in my usual armchair for my afternoon nap. In the past, Trixie would have jumped up to sit on my lap and have a snooze with me and I missed that companionship so badly.

No sooner had I settled down that day than I felt a familiar weight on my lap, as if Trixie was there. I couldn't see her but I could feel the warmth of her body through my skirt and I thought I could sense the movement of her breathing. Feeling very comforted, I nodded off. When I woke up an hour later, the weight had gone, but I looked down and two of Trixie's silvery-white hairs were visible on my skirt. It was the loveliest feeling because I knew for sure I wasn't alone any more.

Now Trixie joins me every afternoon when I have a nap, and I know that one day soon when it is my time to die, she will be waiting for me on the other side.

When Edith came to me for a reading, I could see Trixie walking beside her as she came in the door. 'What a beautiful Scottie!' I remarked, and her eyes filled with tears. 'Is she with me?' she asked, and I was able to tell her that Trixie is with her all the time.

I often see pets with their owners when they come for a reading. One regular client always has a German shepherd lying with his head on her lap.

It's such a strong bond between pet and owner that they will usually reincarnate together. Perhaps the animal might be a different species but not necessarily. All animals are part of a chain and have souls, just as we do, and they live through many different lives, evolving as they go along.

Sleeping with Slippers

Just as we mourn our pets, so they mourn us as well, and they watch out for our spirits returning to comfort them.

After my wife died, her little Jack Russell, name of Jack, used to sleep with her slippers in his bed. At first I kept removing them, but he seemed distressed when they weren't there and came to fetch them back so I decided to let him keep them. He wasn't chewing them to bits as he did with all his toys. In fact, he took very good care of them. When I was sitting in the lounge he would come in and put the slippers in front of the chair where my wife used to sit then he'd look up, almost as if she was still there.

A month after her death, my daughter came to help me clear out my wife's toiletries and she discovered that her makeup bag was missing. We couldn't imagine where it might have gone until we checked in Jack's bed and there, deep down in the midst of his blankets, we found the makeup bag and my wife's hairbrush as well. I took the bag away but decided to let him keep the hairbrush. Later on, we were sitting eating a meal when we heard a peculiar sound. We went through to Jack's basket and saw that he was rolling backwards and forwards on the brush, as if brushing his own coat in the way my wife used to do.

After that, when he brought her slippers into the lounge he would bring the hairbrush as well and place it carefully on the chair. As I watched him, over time, I realised that Jack could see my wife's spirit in that chair and was bringing her the things he thought she would need. He was trying to look after her in death as he had in life.

Jack could see his mummy's spirit even though her husband couldn't. He could probably hear and smell her as well when she came back to comfort her family after death, and he was determined to have her things ready and waiting for her.

By the Graveside

You probably know the story of Greyfriars Bobby, the Skye terrier who kept watch over his master's grave in Edinburgh for fourteen years, leaving only briefly when he needed to get food. He won't have been sitting there for nothing. His master's spirit will have been there with him, and they will have kept each other company through the long cold winter nights. I heard another story of a dog that kept watch over a grave, this time about a golden retriever called Lucy.

While my husband Simon was ill with cancer, Lucy only left his bedside when she needed the toilet. Otherwise she ate all her meals there, slept there, and sat patiently keeping him company all day, even refusing to go out for her usual walks. After he died, at first Lucy lay on his bed or sat on his chair downstairs, barely moving at all and obviously deeply depressed.

Five months after Simon's death, Lucy went missing. I searched everywhere and put up posters round the neighbourhood but couldn't find her. Four days later, I went up to the cemetery to visit Simon's grave and there was Lucy lying beside it. She was very thin and obviously hadn't eaten for four days, but her tail was wagging and she was moving her head in an odd way. It took me a while before I realised what she was doing. She used to nudge our hands when she wanted to be stroked, then bob her head when she got her own way. She was making the same nudging and bobbing movements now, as if Simon was stroking her again.

I took her home with me and fed her but from then on whenever I went up to the grave I took Lucy along and she always moved her head in that distinctive way. I'm convinced she was being stroked by my husband's spirit.

I'm convinced too. There had obviously been a very deep love between Lucy and Simon and death could not break that bond.

The Dog Who Knew

Animals can bring enormous comfort when we are sad. I believe they often sense sad events before we do and will stick by our side, almost feeling our sadness for us. Here's a tale of one lady called Patricia and her little Yorkshire terrier Betty.

One day, out of the blue, Betty went berserk. She started running round the sitting room, barking and crying, going round in circles, dashing to the front door and back again, then lying in front of it with her legs in the air. She wouldn't let me pick her up, and finally she seemed so distressed I decided that she must be in pain and rang the vet. They asked me a few questions and couldn't understand what was going on either but they said to bring her down to the surgery.

I decided to wait for my husband, who was due home shortly, because it would be hard to get Betty into the car in this state and calm her down enough to sit still for the journey. But the time came and went when my husband was due back. I called his office and they said he had left at the usual time, but an hour later he wasn't back.

Betty was still behaving very oddly and I was trying to decide whether to take her to the vet's on my own when the doorbell rang. A policewoman was standing outside. She told me she was very sorry but my husband had been killed in a car accident on his way home. He had died at the scene. When I worked out the time it had happened, I realised it must have been exactly at that moment when Betty first started going berserk in the sitting room. She knew before I did.

The accident happened several miles away, and the only way Betty could have known it had happened was because she was told by angels. She had a very strong psychic sense and I know she was able to communicate with Patricia's husband after death.

Sophie and Skye

I'm afraid this next story always makes me tearful, so bear with me! The family are good friends of mine so I knew Sophie well and often saw the evidence of her incredible bond with her horse, Skye. Here's her story, as told by her mum.

My daughter Sophie battled cancer for over a year, but it became clear that it was a battle she wasn't going to win. We brought her home to nurse her through the last weeks, and during that period her horse Skye began to behave very oddly. She would barge wildly at the doors of the stable and, when we let her out, she would run full tilt into the fence in the field, causing nasty cuts on her chest. No one could seem to stop her.

The day before Sophie died, she asked if she could be carried outside to see her horse one last time. When she saw the cuts, we had to tell her what had happened, then we lifted her up so she could have a last private chat with Skye. She whispered that she would come back to see her and that it wasn't the end, and they both had tears in their eyes. I didn't think horses could cry but it certainly looked that way. Skye licked Sophie and nuzzled her face, and it was an incredibly moving scene. Finally, Sophie said 'She wants us to go now so that she can be sad on her own.'

Sophie passed away peacefully at 10.40 the next morning. Just before that, at 10.35, Skye started neighing really loudly. We heard her from our seats at Sophie's bedside and realised that was her way of saying good-bye.

Our beautiful daughter died just twenty-one days short of her seventeenth birthday. On her birthday we all had some cake and gave Skye an apple, then we sang 'Happy Birthday'. Skye had been quiet and lethargic since Sophie's death but now she neighed seven times, as if joining in the birthday greetings.

We believe that Sophie often visits Skye now. We can leave the gate to the field open and she never comes out, but stands still in the spot where Sophie used to saddle her. Sometimes she does what appears to be a dressage presentation all on her own. Watching her, though, I don't think she's alone at all.

I've got no doubt that Skye and Sophie's bond will continue after death and that if they reincarnate they will come back together. They were both gentle, loving souls who gave so much to each other that their lives were lit up by their relationship.

The Gas Leak

There are countless stories of animals raising the alarm when their owners are in danger. Dogs have a stronger sense of smell than us and they can hear things that are outside the range of human hearing. Cats have better eyesight in the dark, and many other animals have heightened senses, developed to help them survive in the wild. They feel loyalty to their owners, the people who feed them, so it's only natural they would want to help us when they think we might be in danger.

But in the following stories, none of the rational explanations seem to apply. It's hard to see how the animals could possibly have known what was about to happen – unless, of course, they were warned themselves by angels.

I was on my way home from work one day and had just turned into my road when my tabby cat Charlie appeared in front of me, snarling and acting very strangely, in a way that was completely out of character. Every time I tried to walk onwards, he swerved in front of me until it was obvious he wanted to stop me walking any further. I bent down and picked him up, but he struggled to get free, leapt out of my arms and stood in front of me again, blocking my way.

'This is ridiculous,' I said out loud. 'I just want to get into my house after a long day. What's the problem?'

But as I was speaking, I realised there must be something wrong. Charlie must have a reason for behaving this way. Maybe he had seen an intruder breaking into the house and they were still in there?

A retired policeman lived next door so I asked him if he would take my keys, go in and have a look around for me. I sat down on the grass in front of the house and Charlie purred and rubbed himself against me, obviously pleased that I had heeded his warning.

Suddenly, my neighbour came running out. 'Quick!' he yelled. 'Call the gas board! There's a gas leak in the kitchen.'

We called the gas board and managed to find the outside tap to shut the gas off before they arrived. As I was doing this, I sniffed the air deeply, wondering if Charlie had possibly smelled gas and that's why he had known to warn me, but there wasn't a hint of it outside in the garden. My neighbour agreed with me. The windows had been closed all day and I didn't have a cat flap so Charlie couldn't get back into the house until I got home to let him in.

When the gas technicians went into the house, they found there was a defective part in my boiler and they told me it could have blown up at any moment, when it was ignited by the flame of my pilot light. I'd had an incredibly lucky escape.

'How did Charlie know there was something wrong?' my neighbour asked.

I couldn't answer him. When I thought about it later, I could only assume that he had been warned by angels.

It's perhaps more common to hear stories of dogs alerting their owners to danger but cats are perfectly capable of it as well, when the angels warn them.

The Faulty Toaster

Here's another story of a cat preventing what could have been a fatal accident:

I was getting ready for bed one night as usual, having locked up downstairs and turned all the lights off. Normally my cat Echo would have gone out hunting by then – she's the scourge of the local mouse population – but instead, she sat outside my bedroom door and started howling.

I opened the door. 'What's up, Echo? Are you ill?' The noise was so loud I thought maybe there was something wrong with her but she seemed fine, apart from her loud howling.

'Do you want to play?' I asked and flicked the cord of my dressing gown towards her, which usually initiates a game of tug of war. Not this time. She just stood in the doorway howling.

I tried to pick her up but she wriggled out of my grasp, shot towards the top of the stairs and waited for me to follow. When I didn't come immediately she returned to the bedroom door, howled even louder then led me to the top of the stairs.

Eventually I got the message and followed her out to the stairs, then down to the kitchen. As I walked into the room, I couldn't see anything amiss at first but I smelled a faint smell of burning plastic. I searched all round the units until at last I tracked it down. Something seemed to be wrong with the toaster plug, because I could hear a faint crackling coming from it. I tried to unplug it but the plug was burning hot to the touch.

Just then I noticed my next-door neighbour's light was on so I went over to ask his advice. As he unplugged the toaster for me a huge spark shot out, and he told me that if I had left it like that overnight it could have caused an electrical fire. What's more, my bedroom was directly above the kitchen so if a fire had started I could have been in real danger.

When an electrician came the next day, he told me that the wiring was badly worn and could have caught fire at any time. I'd never have known if it wasn't for my remarkable cat Echo.

It's possible that Echo had smelled the burning plastic of the plug, but how would a cat know that it was dangerous? I'm sure angels must have warned Echo and told her to warn her owner. It's the only possible explanation.

Preventing a Road Accident

All animals are spiritual creatures – even goldfish and houseflies. We tend to be more aware of angelic interventions with the larger animals, such as cats, dogs and horses, because we know what is normal behaviour for them and when they are doing something out of the ordinary. Personally, I wouldn't have much idea about abnormal goldfish behaviour!

A client told me the following story about her teenage daughter Erica, who was out riding her horse one day.

Erica had been riding since she was tiny and I had no doubts about her safety on the quiet country roads near our home, especially since her horse, Prince, was such a sensible creature. However, one day she came home very shaken and described to me what had just happened.

She was riding down a particularly narrow lane when suddenly Prince pulled into the gateway to a field and refused point blank to move. She yanked on the reins and kicked her heels, urging him to go forwards, but to no avail. He wasn't budging. It was a warm, cloud-free afternoon and so quiet and still that she could hear the noise of a bumblebee in the hedgerow and the wind brushing through the long grass. What on earth was she going to do if her horse refused to take her any further? This was completely out of character.

All of a sudden, a huge juggernaut came hurtling round a bend up ahead. It was almost as wide as the road, and if she and Prince had been just a little bit further on it would have been unable to avoid them on the single-track lane. Erica realised that Prince had saved her life, but she couldn't work out how he could possibly have known the juggernaut was coming. She had heard nothing but the sounds of nature.

Once she got over her anger that such a huge vehicle should be speeding along country lanes, my client decided to mention the story to me, because it seemed to her the only explanation was that an angel had been guiding Prince at the time.

I know horses have sensitive hearing, but Erica had waited several minutes in the entrance to that field without detecting any sign of an oncoming vehicle. I'm convinced my client is right and that an angel saved her daughter's life that day by telling Prince to stay in the entrance to the field until the danger had passed.

Judo the German Shepherd

I once had a dog called Judo who was an angel here on earth, sent to help other animals and humans. He was friends with everyone in the neighbourhood and liked to wander round socialising. He sometimes went out with our neighbour, who was a policeman, or followed the postman on his rounds, or went to watch play on the village cricket pitch.

One day, when Judo was eight, the postman left the gate open and Judo walked down the road to the recreation ground. A woman with a baby in a pushchair and two toddlers alongside her was waiting to cross the road, and Judo sat down on the pavement beside them. The little girl was fidgeting and her mother kept admonishing her to hold onto the pushchair, but suddenly she let go and stepped into the road. Quick as a flash, Judo leapt in front of the little girl and nudged her back to the pavement just as a car came speeding along. The car hit him on the head, but the little girl's life was saved.

Judo managed to stagger onto the cricket pitch, where he collapsed and died of a fractured skull. Everyone knew him there so they came to fetch me. My lovely dog died a hero, just as he was meant to do. He knew when he sat down on the pavement that little girl was going to step into the path of an oncoming car. That's why he sat down beside her.

I've always believed that animals know far more than we give them credit for. Judo was extraordinarily intelligent and sensitive, a dog who lit up all of our lives.

Angels in the Wild

Just as there are good and bad people, so there are good and bad animals. Some can be aggressive, selfish and jealous, while others, like Judo, are angels here on earth. I keep coming across stories of heroic, altruistic behaviour in the animal world that no naturalist can explain. It's understandable that animals would save others of their own species, because that may help their own survival, but why would they save other species – or human beings?

It's quite common to hear stories of dolphins saving humans from a shark attack, but it actually happened to an American friend of mine, Rita, and it was a life-changing experience for her.

We took our boat out in the Gulf of Mexico and I decided to have a quick swim because it was such a hot day. I knew there were sharks out there but we had a good look around and couldn't see any, and the water looked so enticing that I decided to risk it.

I had swum a little bit away from the boat when two dolphins appeared and started frolicking around me. I thought they wanted to play and was delighted. One of them let me hold his fin and pulled me through the water towards the boat. That's when I heard my husband shouting. I looked up and saw him waving his arms frantically in the air.

'Get out of the water!' he was yelling. 'Quick! Hurry!'

I scrambled to the steps of the boat, accompanied by my dolphin friends. My husband hauled me up and I noticed he was shaking as he pointed to the place where I had been a few minutes earlier. A huge bull shark – about ten feet long – was circling, his dorsal fin clearly visible above the surface.

'Those dolphins held him back until you got out of the water,' my husband told me. 'They saved your life.'

And I thought they had just been playing! I looked out to where my dolphins were disappearing off towards the horizon and blew them a kiss of gratitude before my knees gave way beneath me. I'm a very spiritual person and I believe angels got those dolphins to save me that day – but I won't ever risk swimming out there again. I've had my warning.

On Safari

Some friends of mine filmed a wildlife series for television and they told me some incredible stories of animal behaviour in Africa that their experts said were unprecedented.

Elephants and rhinos don't mix. They're not the best of friends and in fact elephants have been known to kill rare rhino species where their territories overlap or abut each other. That's why we couldn't believe our eyes when we saw two elephants standing side by side all day long with a young rhino. 'What are they doing?' we kept asking each other. 'What's going on?' What was even stranger was that these two were teenagers, and teenage elephants are prone to huge mood swings in the same way that human teenagers are. Male elephants are at their most aggressive in their teens.

As evening fell, the three started walking together towards a watering hole about half a mile away. The rhino walked between the elephants, occasionally swerving sideways and bumping against one of them.

'There's something wrong with that rhino,' we commented, and then one guy finally worked it out. 'She's blind!' he exclaimed. 'The elephants are helping her to the watering hole.'

None of us have ever seen the like in our entire professional careers, but that's definitely what was happening.

Here's another story from a different film crew:

A lioness approached our 4 x 4 and rubbed her head against it then looked up at us. We were wary because we knew this individual had cubs and would defend them aggressively if we went anywhere near her den. She walked six paces ahead of us then turned back and looked.

'She wants us to follow,' my cameraman said, astonished. 'She's acting like a domestic cat or dog that wants you to go with them.'

We followed and she led us across the plain and into a clearing where a sight of carnage awaited us. There had been some kind of attack and a lioness was lying dead on the ground with a cub dead beside her, while two other cubs who were still alive kept nudging her to get up. Our lioness had brought us here to see this. Once she knew we had seen the cubs, she turned and left, obviously expecting us to look after them, which we did.

But once again, it is completely out of a lioness's nature to try to save another lioness's cubs. It's just not something they do because the cubs will be in competition with theirs for food and territory. Except that this one did.

Whenever animals behave in a way that is out of character in order to do good for other creatures, I am convinced that there are angels involved and that they intervened for a reason. The men on that film shoot were seasoned wildlife experts and they couldn't explain the behaviour in any other way.

My Family's Psychic Pets

I've only got one pet at the moment – Henry, my elderly blind cat. There have been umpteen cats, dogs and horses over the years, though, all of them quite different characters who were psychic in their own different ways.

There was Carla, a Labrador-Doberman cross, who used to look after Henry and make sure he didn't bump into things. They would nuzzle heads together and were the best of friends. Carla adored my grandson Thomas and seemed to know instinctively when he was coming for a visit, even if we hadn't said anything. She'd go out and sit by the gate with a ball in her mouth, waiting for Thomas to arrive and give her a game. Then when my husband Michael went into hospital for an operation, Carla sat at the door peering up the drive until he returned. She wouldn't go out to play or come and snuggle with me on the sofa because she didn't want to abandon her post.

Since Carla died, she has visited me several times, most recently when Nicky was in hospital. I was lying on my bed, looked up, and there was Carla gazing at me. I said 'You OK?' and she wagged her tail. The next time I saw her I bent down to stroke her out of sheer force of habit, but she had gone. 'It's good to see you again,' I told her. I knew she was visiting me to cheer me up during a very stressful time when Nicky was seriously ill (more about that in the next chapter), and it definitely helped to see her lovely face.

Another dog, Barney, was totally scatty – the kind of dog who chases his own tail and buries his bones then can't find them later – but he often saw spirits before I did. He didn't bark at them but I'd find him staring into the corner and I'd look myself and see who he was look-ing at.

I've always found that I can communicate with animals, in the same way I do with disabled children, by opening my mind and listening. Sometimes, I am able to pass messages to owners from their pets. They tell me how they are being treated, why they're not doing some-thing, or when they are in pain. I can't go to zoos any more because it's too upsetting walking round hearing all these captive beasts telling me how unhappy they are in their cages. When I'm walking down the street I often have conversations with passing animals but I have to do it subtly or people would think I'd gone completely loopy. I just say a quick 'hello, how are you?' in my head!

My daughter Tanya has a genuine affinity with animals: she loves them and they love her. She used to have a horse called Musky and she could be inside the house and say his name in a normal voice – 'I'm just going out to see Musky' – and we'd look out the window and he'd be running across the field to the point where they always greeted each other. He knew whenever she was coming because they had a strong psychic connection.

Tanya had other horses over the years and she was close to all of them. When she was sixteen, she had a very difficult decision to make – one that faces most pet owners at some time or another.

My horse Lady, a beautiful bay thoroughbred, had botulism poisoning, along with three other horses in the stables. It's a horrific disorder caused when they ingest toxic bacteria from soil or water, and it has a high fatality rate in horses. When I arrived to visit her, I was told one of the other horses had just died. I went in to Lady's stable and sat with her head in my lap, trying my best to soothe her, but she was thrashing from side to side. It was horrible to watch but I didn't want to leave her suffering like this, so in my head I asked what I should do.

When the reply came, I knew it was Lady speaking to me. 'Help me, help me, let me go,' she said.

I went to find the vet, who was treating another sick horse. 'I've done all I can for her,' he said. 'It's only a matter of time, unless you want to hasten things a bit. It's up to you.'

It was the biggest decision I'd ever been asked to make in my young life, but I knew I had to let her go. That's what she wanted and I couldn't be selfish about it.

I held Lady's head, stroking her, as the vet gave her the injection. She looked into me – right into me – and I heard the words 'Thank you, thank you.' I felt a huge rush of love for her and I felt her love coming back to me as the pain eased and her life ebbed away. I'll never forget that moment as long as I live.

Through her relationships with her horses, Tanya learned never to take animals for granted. She always asks a horse if she can ride it before getting on, and like me, she is prone to chatting to cats and dogs she passes in the street.

All animals are psychic, without exception. They use their senses far more than we do, and sense danger in a way we never can (unless we have been warned by angels). Domestic pets put their owners before themselves, just as police dogs and guide dogs always put their handlers first. They even remain loyal to their owners if they are mistreated. They have an intelligence deriving from their psychic abilities that we don't always recognise. Watch a guide dog waiting to alert a blind person when the bus reaches their stop, or a disabled person's pet predicting what they will need before they've thought of it themselves, and you'll see what I mean.

Never underestimate your pet and the strength of the bond you have with them, because I know for a fact that they become angels who come back to watch over us after death. And many are angels who look after us in life as well.

Chapter 7

Healing Angels

One of the times when we need angels the most is when we, or someone close to us, is ill or in pain. We feel very vulnerable when we place ourselves in the hands of doctors or nurses, who may not have the time to sit and explain everything to us at length. Hospitals are alien places full of unfamiliar machines, antiseptic smells and a faceless bureaucracy, and doctors' consulting rooms often aren't much better. We might struggle to express ourselves clearly when we are feeling poorly, and with some doctors you feel as though you are being rushed out the door to make way for the next patient. It is at times like this that angels can really provide comfort.

I know what I'm talking about because I've had my fair share of health problems over the years. In chapter 1, I mentioned the pulmonary embolism I suffered when Carl was ten, Nicky was nine and Tanya was seven years old. I woke in the middle of the night with an agonising pain in my chest, struggling to breathe, and I was utterly petrified, even after I heard my mother's voice telling me

I would be OK. As I lay in the hospital ward waiting for treatment, angels came to me and calmed me down, teaching me a kind of self-hypnosis technique that eased the pain. The nurses were amazed because when they next came to check on me, my heart rate had slowed down and my breathing was much easier. I told them I didn't need the painkillers they'd brought me any more and they nearly fell over backwards in surprise because embolisms are notoriously painful.

It was just as well that I learned those pain-relief techniques, because I've had five more embolisms since then. I suffer from a condition called thrombophilia – the opposite of haemophilia – which means that my blood clots too easily, causing embolisms and strokes. I take medication for it, but this will almost certainly be what kills me one day. I don't know when, and I have chosen not to go for a long time yet, but I am not worried about dying. It's the letting go that is hard for some people, but I have died already and I know that it is a beautiful experience.

I've spoken to lots of people who have died and come back again because it wasn't their time, and their stories are all remarkably similar. In my case, I was having an emergency hysterectomy in my twenties and, while on the operating table, I remember floating through a dark place towards a door that was slightly ajar. There was golden light streaming round the edges of the door and it sounded as though there was a lively party in full swing on the other side. I knew my mother would be in there, because she had passed over by then, and I reached my arms out towards the door, trying to get in.

'You have to go back. It is not your time. We are not ready for you,' a man's voice said clearly.

I felt absolute, total disappointment at not being able to go through the door. I didn't look backwards at that point and remember that I was a married woman with three young children who would have been desperately upset if I had died. I wasn't worried about anything left behind on the earth. All I could think about was getting to that golden light. But it wasn't to be – not then.

Next, I found myself on the ceiling of the operating theatre looking down as doctors tried to restart my heart. The wound in my abdomen where they had removed my womb was still open and they were apply-ing paddles to my chest then standing back as electric shocks made my body convulse. I could hear what they were saying, although I didn't understand much of it because they were talking about technical measurements they were reading from the dials.

After that, I remember nothing more until I woke up in the recovery room. I mumbled to the nurse who was keeping an eye on me: 'I died, didn't I?'

'No, no. You didn't,' she said, then looked embarrassed. 'I'd better get the doctor to have a word with you about that.'

The doctor wouldn't admit it to me but my husband found out from a young nurse that that's exactly what had happened. Seemingly I was too anaemic and shouldn't have been operated on at that time because my blood count was too low and my heart just stopped mid-operation.

Once I got over the shock of having died, I felt very calm and comforted. I know now that I will be warned when it is my time, and I know that it will be a peaceful, happy experience. Since then, I have told my story to several other people who have had near-death experiences and they all say 'Yes, that's exactly what happened to me.' They know the feeling.

The Man in White

Before her death, my mother once told me about an angel who came to her during an operation. She suffered from tuberculosis and had to have one of her lungs removed.

I remember the rubber mask over my face and the surgeon starting to count backwards from ten and I definitely became unconscious for a while but part way through the operation I woke up. I couldn't open my eyes but I could hear the doctors and nurses talking to each other. I wasn't in pain but I could feel them doing something in my chest, which was quite terrifying and I started to panic. I wanted to let them know I was awake, but I couldn't speak and had no way of signalling to them.

And then a man all in white appeared and stood alongside the operating table and held my hand. I knew straight away that he was an angel because he had a kind of glow about him and he instantly made me feel warm and peaceful. I loved the sensation of his hand holding mine.

'Is it okay to go back to sleep?' I asked him.

He nodded to me, so I did – I went back to sleep again, and when I woke up after the operation he had gone.

My mother was very ill but she said that as soon as she saw the angel she knew she would survive. He didn't have to say anything. He made her feel good just by being there.

The Angel's Voice

There is a time for us to live and a time for us to die, and even after we have an accident, or get cancer or some other life-threatening illness, angels can step in and help us if we are destined to spend longer in this lifetime. An American lady called Sue told me the following story about her own near-death experience.

I don't remember anything about the car accident. I've got no idea how it happened. I didn't see the truck coming and I felt nothing on impact. The world just went black. Then I heard some voices.

'This one's dead,' a man's voice said. His fingers were on my neck and I realised with a shock that he was talking about me. How ridiculous!

'Put a blanket on top of her and come and help over here,' a woman's voice told him.

'Stop! Don't go!' I was thinking in my head, but I realised the words weren't coming out. I knew I wasn't dead yet but I must have been on the point of dying because the emergency services had been unable to detect any vital signs.

And then an angel arrived. I couldn't see anything but I knew there was an angel present because I instantly felt an incredible sense of calmness, as if there was a protective cloak around me.

'You are not coming with me,' the angel said. 'You are staying where you are.'

Suddenly I heard the words 'I am here.' The strange thing was, my mouth was open and the words were coming out of it but I knew it wasn't me saying it. It wasn't my voice. Don't ask me how, but I just knew the angel was speaking through me. 'I am here,' it said again.

I heard the man's voice saying 'Oh my God, that woman is alive after all. Quick!'

I felt fingers feeling for the pulse in my neck and then I lapsed into unconsciousness. When I woke up again I was in a hospital bed with plaster casts all over me and drips coming out of my arm. I could remember the angel perfectly and I know that he saved my life that day by using my voice to ask for help. There's no doubt about it in my mind.

When angels speak through us there is never any doubt that it is coming from them. When it happens to me, it is always a very clear voice that either sounds as if it is coming from inside my head or from someone standing right beside me. It doesn't sound like my voice at all. Whyever not? Angels are also able to use our voiceboxes when they need to bypass our minds and get through to us clearly or quickly. This makes it less surprising that they can take control of someone's accelerator foot in a car, or lift someone bodily back from a cliff edge. They can do what they want with our bodies – even heal them from illness. Whatever they do with us is always helpful and positive.

X Marks the Spot

A woman called Sally came to me in great distress because she had just been diagnosed as having an inoperable brain tumour. She was a mother to two children aged nine and eleven and terrified of having to leave them.

'I can't die!' she sobbed to me over and over again. 'No one else will look after them as well as I would. They need me.'

I closed my eyes and in my head I asked for help from God and Jesus on this woman's behalf. The message I got back was that she had to ask the angels herself and all would be well. I explained this to her and calmed her down a little bit before she left. I'll let her take up the story.

It was unimaginably horrible when my tumour was diagnosed. They showed it to me on the scan so I had an image in my head of this toxic mass pressing against my brain, getting bigger all the time. I felt like a walking time bomb. The worst thing was that there was nothing I could do about it except take the medication they prescribed. If you have a cold you can take lots of vitamin C and keep warm and rest, and I wanted someone to tell me what you can do for a brain tumour – but no one could. Then when

Dorothy advised me to pray, I felt a little better because at least that was something I could try myself.

I began praying to the angels several times every day. They were never far from my thoughts. I asked my mother and grandmother, who had passed over, if they would intervene on my behalf, and I prayed to Jesus and God and anyone I could think of.

I often pictured the tumour in my head and I started imagining it shrinking, trying to impose my will on it. Sometimes when I prayed, I thought I could make out a voice saying 'You will be fine' but I wanted to hear these words so much that I couldn't convince myself I wasn't making them up. It might just be wishful thinking.

Six weeks later, I was called in to hospital for a follow-up brain scan and I could tell from the doctor's and radiographer's faces that they expected the tumour to be significantly bigger. They spoke to me carefully, in subdued tones, and I wondered if they were expecting my cognitive abilities to be affected already. I lay down on the scanner and held still as I was conveyed inside the huge, humming machinery.

I seemed to be in the scanner for longer than usual and when I came out again, there was no mistaking the expressions of astonishment in the room.

'What's happened?' I asked, scared it meant a serious turn for the worse.

'We can't find your tumour any more. It's not where it was. In fact, it's gone,' the radiographer told me. 'I've never seen anything like this in all the years I've been working.'

My knees buckled under me and I had to sit down for a moment to take in the news.

'We're just going to print out the films and then the doctor will have a look at them with you.'

In the consulting room, the doctor frowned at the film. 'There's no sign of a tumour but look – what on earth is that?'

I peered along with him. In the spot where the tumour used to be, there was a tiny X.

'That must be a mark on the film,' he said, but when he looked at the scan on his computer screen, the X was there too. 'Well, I never,' he said, rubbing his chin thoughtfully. 'I've got no idea what could have caused that.'

I decided not to tell him about the angels. I could sense he was too much of a black-and-white scientist to believe me. But I know for sure that angels cured my brain tumour and I can't thank them enough.

I think Sally should have told her doctor about the angels. She might have found he had had an angel experience himself, and at the very least she could have started the process of opening his mind to angels. Many doctors I speak to are very spiritual people who have daily conversations with their own angels as they search for the best way to help their sick patients.

A Visit from an Archangel

If you believe, and then ask the angels for help in the right way, you *will* be heard. I heard the following story from a client of mine called Izabella about her experience with breast cancer.

In the summer of 2001 while I was on a shamanic training course I found a small lump in my right breast. Within three days the lump had doubled in size so I hurried along to my doctor's surgery. A few days later I had a biopsy and in another week I saw the breast surgeon, who booked me in to have surgery just a couple of weeks hence.

The shaman I was studying with believed he could get rid of the lump without surgery and a week before the operation I started an intensive course of daily healing with him. I felt myself pulled in two directions. Should I take the natural alternative way or follow the more drastic conventional approach? During that time I was also attending a meditation group once a week and in the course of the final meditation before surgery I had one of the most profound experiences of my life.

Suddenly before me there rose a man wearing a suit of armour with wings sprouting from his shoulder blades. He stood right in front of me, almost touching me. I was overwhelmed by his strength, power and passion – and his rage.

'This was not meant to happen,' he said angrily, 'but it is moving too fast now so you must have it removed and accept all the treatment available. You will be saved. We will protect you and support you. But it is too late and you must go through all the treatment.' He said again, 'We missed this. It shouldn't have happened.' He sounded passionate but extremely protective.

After he left I was literally speechless. I went to consult someone I knew who would be able to explain who he was and she told me that I had seen the Archangel Michael. She gave me a picture of him that was exactly the same as the image in my head. After that I had no doubts about what I was meant to do.

When my breast was removed and biopsied, they found the cancer was an extremely aggressive one, even more so than they had realised. I had to go through a year of treatment, more than the average, and I never doubted or wavered. No matter how sick I was or how difficult it was to keep going, I knew it was the right thing to do.

To this day I believe Archangel Michael saved my life by giving me the advice he did and strengthening my faith that all would be well in the end, and I am extremely grateful.

Izabella was already a very spiritual person – that's why she was doing a shamanic training course – and she is also a very strong woman. I know she had a horrible year on repeated courses of chemo and radiotherapy that made her lose her hair, throw up continually and feel completely at rock bottom some days, but she never lost her faith that she would get better with the angels' help. And I'm delighted that she has now been clear of cancer for seven years.

The Power of Prayer

I don't want to imply that everyone who has cancer will be cured if they just pray hard enough, because life isn't like that. If it is your time to die, then it will happen, but prayer can make the final days, weeks or months easier for you by offering the comfort that you will not make that last journey alone. The angels will be by your side.

As I mentioned earlier, there are two possible times when we can die. A teenage girl called Ruby was diagnosed with terminal cancer. The family weren't very spiritual and her mother only came to see me in desperation after Ruby had lapsed into unconsciousness and the family were told she had only a few days to live. During the reading, I could see it was touch and go and that Ruby was very close to going over, but I advised her mother to pray with all her heart and soul, from a place very deep within her. Here's what happened next.

I don't know what made me go to see Dorothy. A friend had told me about her years before but in Ruby's last days I was just clutching at straws. I don't think I really believed she would be able to help but I knew that I had to try everything humanly possible to save my little girl.

I'd been 'praying' ever since Ruby was first diagnosed, but in retrospect I was just paying lip service. 'Please God, don't let her die' is not enough. After talking to Dorothy I started praying with my heart and soul and my whole being. I sat by my daughter's bedside watching the slight rise and fall of her chest and the chalk-white colour of her skin and I prayed with everything I had.

'Take me instead. Take everything I own. Just please save my baby.' Tears were streaming down my cheeks as I sat up all night holding Ruby's hand and watching her lying in very deep sleep. Towards morning, I think I dozed off briefly and I had a dream. Nothing particularly happened in it that I can remember but I woke up with a warm feeling that everything was going to be all right. I had no reason to think this, but I felt peaceful and blissfully happy. Yet the reality was that I was still sitting by my daughter's deathbed.

As light began to stream round the edges of the blinds, I looked at Ruby closely and wasn't sure at first if it was just my imagination or if she had more colour in her cheeks. Her breathing sounded more natural as well.

A nurse came in to check up on her and commented that she looked better. 'But please don't get your hopes up,' she added. 'Sometimes patients have a last burst of energy before they pass away.'

An hour later, Ruby and I were alone in the room together when she opened her eyes and looked at me for the first time in days.

'Hello darling,' I whispered, smiling at her. 'How are you feeling?'

'I'm hungry,' she said. 'Is there anything to eat?'

My heart leapt. She hadn't asked for food for a long time now. We'd been having to force her to swallow a few mouthfuls just to keep her alive. I rang for a nurse, who looked surprised but brought her a bowl of soup, and she gulped down every spoonful until it was gone.

'Is there any more?' she asked, and I wanted to jump for joy. I knew in my heart this was a turning point.

The nurse called a doctor and he too cautioned me against getting my hopes up but took some blood tests all the same. When the results came back, they couldn't believe their eyes because all traces of the cancer had gone. It was an astounding miracle.

Ruby had to stay in hospital for a while longer to get her strength back and they ran loads of tests on her trying to work out what had happened and how she had recovered from terminal cancer. I told them I believed it was the power of prayer that had saved her and could see from the raised eyebrows they thought I was crazy, but I knew it was true. If I hadn't prayed from deep within me that night, it could well have been Ruby's last.

When I did the reading for Ruby's mother I knew that Ruby could have died that death. Her illness happened for a reason, to help her parents become more spiritual and less materialistic, and I'm glad to say they learned that life lesson. They were a wealthy couple with big houses, smart cars and all the trappings that money can buy, but since Ruby's illness they have given a lot to charity and the mother now works as a volunteer with the homeless. They have learned what is truly important – and Ruby will live a long life instead of a short one.

The Power to Move

Illness is a very lonely place. No matter how close your friends and family are, only you know the secret fears in your head, the anxiety you feel over each new symptom and the terror about what the future holds. Some people live with intolerable pain, day in and day out, and have to find the strength to keep going. Whether they know it or not, angels are with them all the time, helping them through, but there are still days when they are cast down into the depths of despair.

When you have a serious health problem for which the medical establishment can offer no cure, the future can look very bleak. All your priorities change. Instead of dreaming that you will write an award-winning novel or compose a symphony, you just hope to get through the next hour without crying, or being sick, or hunching over in pain. Everything contracts into the present moment and what is happening to your body, and you can't always think clearly in this state.

Jane was happily married with a young family when a catastrophic road accident caused a spinal problem that left her paralysed from the neck down.

Straight after the accident I still had hope that I would be able to walk again. If it were at all possible, I was determined I would do it by working as hard as I could at my physiotherapy, because kids need an active mum. But as the weeks went by and it became clear things weren't improving, I sank into gloom. They sent me back to live at home in the midst of my family, with carers coming in and out to deal with all the messy bits like toilet functions and feeding tubes. I could talk to my children and my husband, and I could kiss them if they came right up to my lips, but that was all I could do. I couldn't play with them, make meals for them or give them hugs.

As time went on and I realised that this was what the rest of my life was going to be like, I began to think hard. If I died, my husband would be able to remarry and the kids would have someone who could be a proper mum to them – someone who could look after them, instead of them having to look after her. I was totally useless, nothing but a drain on everyone around me. I decided that the unselfish course of action would be for me to take my own life. The only problem was how I could manage that without being able to move. I'd have to persuade someone to help me, but I didn't want them to get into trouble.

That night I prayed that my life could be ended peacefully and that my family would find happiness after I was gone. I meant it with all my heart and soul, and I begged

God to show me a way to make it happen. After I'd finished praying I sank into a sleep that was deeper than I'd had for some time, and when I woke the next morning, I felt a little less depressed. Over the next couple of days, whenever I was on my own I continued to pray for release from my suffering and for my family's happiness.

Since the accident I had often felt sensations in my paralysed body and doctors told me that was quite common because there is a muscle memory in the nerve endings, but that it didn't mean any more than that. But when I woke on the morning of the third day, something unbelievable had happened. I was convinced I could feel my fingers. I focused my mind as hard as I possibly could and with sheer force of will I managed to lift two of the fingers of my right hand up off the blanket.

I called my husband in huge excitement and demonstrated the movement for him, and he was overwhelmed with joy.

The next morning, I could move all of the fingers of my right hand, albeit very slightly. Within a week, I could lift the whole hand and waggle the fingers, and within a month I had regained the use of my right arm – which was amazing because it meant I could hug my children again. The left arm has been a bit slower but it is getting there and meanwhile, I've started to be able to wiggle my toes. I'm still in a wheelchair and fairly helpless at the time of writing to you, but I look forward to each new day because it always seems to bring a slight improvement in my condition.

I'm convinced that angels answered my prayers that night, but instead of giving me the ability to kill myself, they decided it would be best for me and my family if I were to live. I thank them for that every single day, as I chat with my children, help them with their homework and watch them playing together. It would have been totally wrong of me to leave them, and I'm so glad the angels helped me to see that.

It is important to realise that we don't always know best, and what we wish for may not be right for us and those around us. Angels can take a longer view, based on the life lessons we need to learn. They have our best interests at heart. It may sound cruel for all those of you out there who continue to suffer, despite praying from the depths of your being, but there is bound to be a reason for your suffering, a purpose behind it all. Keep praying and one day you will find out what it is for you.

Health Warnings

As well as helping us to cope with ill health, angels can help us to stay healthy and warn us when we risk damaging our health. I've often heard alternative health practitioners exhorting us to 'listen to our bodies'. If we feel tired, we should rest. If we feel like drinking carrot juice, that's what we should do. If we feel stiff, we should stretch. These are the simplest examples I can think of, but the body is a complex, sophisticated organism and we will have 'instincts' about how well it is functioning that are much more subtle than this.

There's that word 'instincts' again! As you know by now, I believe that what we think of as 'instincts' are actually messages from our angels. They might be telling us to slow down, eat more healthy food, say no to that extra glass of wine, or go out for a long walk in the fresh air. If you are sick, they might guide you towards the best type of food to eat or liquid to drink if you listen carefully. And if there's a voice in your head saying 'No!' when a GP prescribes a course of drugs or a surgeon recommends an operation, maybe you should think about getting a second opinion.

When I give readings, I can often spot health problems that clients already have or are heading towards. If I think I can help them to avoid illness, I will give advice. Some people are incredibly grateful – while others simply don't want to know.

About twenty years ago I gave back-to-back readings for two brothers who were reasonably well known in the film business, one as a director and the other as a producer. When the first one, the producer, came in, he had just stubbed out a cigarette and I could smell it very strongly on his clothing. I hate the smell of cigarettes – always have – but I carried on with the reading. Before he left, I said, 'You mustn't smoke another cigarette or it will be your last. If you want to live longer, please stop smoking now.'

He gave a kind of half-smile but didn't comment and I watched as he walked down the corridor, lighting a fresh cigarette before he disappeared round the corner. 'You fool!' I thought to myself. He could have been saved if he had heeded my warning.

I told his brother, the director, what had happened. The brother said 'We've all been worried about him because he can hardly breathe if he tries to climb stairs or walk any distance at all. I've been nagging him to go to the doctor but he won't go.' I said that I hadn't noticed him being breathless.

'No, he's fine when he's sitting down, but as soon as he has to move around, he has big problems.'

After the director left, I had a very uneasy feeling about his brother. My guidance from the angels had been very stark – that he would die if he smoked one more cigarette – and I had seen him light one up in the corridor outside. Sure enough, I got a call the next day to say that the producer had collapsed and died in a coffee bar down the road not long after our meeting.

When I sense that people are close to death like this, I always wonder if there is anything more I should be doing. If it is only their first possible time to die, they could have many more years of life ahead of them, but if it is the second time, there would be nothing I could do anyway. I listen to my angels' guidance and act in the way they suggest. Sometimes this means not telling someone that they are about to die, because the knowledge would be too hard for them to bear and there would be nothing they could do about it anyway. Maybe I will nudge people close to them to make their peace and ensure that everything they want to say has been said, but there are many things in the world that are not meant to be known in advance, and I have to respect that.

The Problem with Drugs

Addictions to nicotine, drugs and alcohol alter our perceptions and mean that it is much harder for angels to get messages through to us. The chemical and psychological hold these substances have over addicts can override everything else, with tragic consequences.

Two years ago, a young man of twenty-three came to see me. I think he had been sent by his mother because he had a serious cocaine habit and she was hoping that I could help. As soon as I spoke to the angels, I received a very stern message indeed.

'If you take so much as one more sniff of a drug for the rest of your life, it will kill you,' I told him. I always tape my sessions with clients and give them a CD to take away with them, and I know the anti-drugs message was reinforced several times on that CD because I kept getting strong warnings from the angels throughout that meeting.

The young man got a real scare that day and I heard from his mother that he gave up the cocaine and all the other drugs straight away and began to sort out his life.

Two years later, he got involved with a new girlfriend who, unbeknown to him at first, occasionally indulged in cocaine. One evening when they were out at a party, she took some and offered her supply to him. 'Go on,' she urged. 'Just one line. What harm can it do?'

I'm sure he will have remembered our session and the warnings I gave him, but two years on, the memory of the high he used to get from cocaine was foremost in his brain and he allowed himself to be talked into it. He snorted a line and seconds later fell to the floor clutching his chest. He died of a massive heart attack before an ambulance could get there.

His mother called me after the funeral. 'We found the CD you made for him,' she said, 'and you couldn't have given him a clearer warning that one more sniff would kill him. It's just a tragedy for his family that his addiction was stronger than his belief in angels.'

He had a choice – and the choice he made was almost like pressing the 'stop' button himself. He will have some big important lessons to learn in his next life before he can evolve any further.

Go to the Doctor!

Some people are a regular fixture in their doctor's waiting room, while others let years go by without a visit. Lots of symptoms we experience in day-to-day life can be attributed to a cause quite easily: indigestion from a late, heavy meal; exhaustion from too many late nights; a calf muscle sprain from wearing high heels too often while charging round town. But we all know that nagging feeling when we get a symptom that we can't understand. If there is a voice in your head saying 'Maybe I should get this checked out,' don't delay. It might turn out to be something minor – or it may well be that the check-up could save your life.

If you leave a doctor's surgery unhappy with the diagnosis and treatment he has prescribed, listen to your instinct and get a second opinion. You've got nothing to lose. Here's what happened to a woman called Heather:

I had a routine mammogram just after my fiftieth birthday and got the all clear. They saw no sign of any problems. About a week later, I was lying in bed unable to sleep when my late husband's voice came into my head, saying really clearly 'Go and get another mammogram.'

My husband was a wonderful man, who had died in a plane crash several years before. I'd spoken to him regularly since then and thought I heard his responses in my head but I had never heard his voice speaking to me out loud like that. It was almost as if he was in the room, repeating 'Get it checked, get it checked.'

'But I've just had it checked,' I told him.

'Get it checked again,' he said.

The next morning I decide to follow his advice, so I went to a private clinic and paid for another mammogram myself. Sure enough, they found a small, early-stage tumour in my left breast.

I felt totally empowered when I went back to my original doctor waving the results of the second mammogram and asking for treatment. The tumour was cancerous but it was caught at such an early stage that they were able to remove it before it spread anywhere else and I was able to keep my breast. I didn't have to have chemotherapy and I only have a tiny scar to show that anything untoward happened.

It made me feel very loved and protected to know that my husband is still looking out for me from beyond the grave. It made me smile as well because he used to love my breasts, and it's nice that he managed to save them!

I don't mean to encourage disrespect for the medical profession. They get things right hundreds more times than they get it wrong. All I want to say is that doctors work very long hours under huge pressure, and it is up to us to take responsibility for our own health. This means listening to the little voices in our heads, paying attention to unusual signs and taking action whenever we are in any doubt; in other words, listening to the angels!

The Seventh Child

A client by the name of Laura told me about a miracle that happened to her French grandmother Charlotte back in 1950 after the birth of her seventh child.

Charlotte gave birth to her seventh child at home, but unfortunately the baby was stillborn as she had *placenta previa* [where the placenta covers the opening to the cervix, making it difficult for the baby to get out]. About a month after the birth, she woke up in a pool of blood and the doctor who was called out said she had gangrene right through her abdomen. The family were well-off and they immediately summoned a specialist from Paris, but his diagnosis was that surgery had a poor chance of success and that the six children should be prepared for their mother to die.

Charlotte was moved to the Clinic of the Virgin Mary in Bourges. Her condition was deteriorating rapidly but she was able to eat half a piece of communion bread. Everyone at the clinic was praying for Charlotte and she decided to have the operation, despite her weakened state and the warnings that it might not succeed. A Parisian surgeon opened her abdomen and found to his amazement that all traces of gangrene had gone and her womb was perfectly healthy.

The miracle changed her. Before she had been too busy to spend much time with her children, but now she saw what was important in life and became a devoted mother and, in time, grandmother. She was so grateful for her life being spared that she carried an aura of love and luck around her. She lived to the age of eighty-nine, by which time she was blind and in a wheelchair, but if anyone asked how she was, she would answer with a beaming smile: 'Really well. And how are you?'

Prayer saved Charlotte's life and gave her children a better mother than they had had before. Eating communion bread and having a religious community praying for you is one way of focusing your prayers to the angels, but there are others, as I'll describe in the next section.

A Network of Prayer

I've had a couple of bad scares with my daughters over the years. In chapter 2, I described the night when Tanya had a severe allergic reaction to ibuprofen and nearly died. We've recently been through another trauma after Nicky had an operation on her pelvis.

Nicky was born in extended breech position – bottom first with her legs up – and it caused a malformation of her pelvis. This meant that one leg was shorter than the other and her pelvis was tilted the wrong way so that the ball rolled around the edge of her hip socket giving her a lot of pain. Fixing it required a huge operation, involving breaking her pelvis in three places, pinning it and bringing it back into alignment. There were six surgeons and she was on the operating table for seven hours while we waited anxiously for news.

When you or someone you love is seriously ill, you want your prayers to be as powerful as they possibly can. What I do is call four or five people around the world – I call it my World Healing Network – and ask them to pray. They spread the word and the energy of prayer comes in to me from around the world. You don't need to use this network, though. It's just one of many approaches that can work. If you know any healers, you can ask them to send healing. If you are religious, go into your church and pray or light a candle. Even throwing coins into a wishing well or putting a message in a bottle can help if you do them with a pure intention. Physical actions can work more effectively than passive wishing in our heads. When we send out a prayer like this, we bring it into sharp focus.

So my Healing Network was praying for Nicky that day as I waited to hear how the operation had gone, but the first word I got was that she had lost five litres of blood on the operating table and was critically ill. It was touch and go whether she would pull through. I felt as though I had been punched in the stomach but I had to pick myself up and try to be strong for the rest of the family, who were standing by, equally anxious. Her husband Mark remained strong and positive throughout, but the experience changed his outlook. I think he prayed deep within his heart and soul. They are such a loving family.

When I was finally allowed to see her, I walked into the recovery ward and there was my mum standing by Nicky's bed with a couple of other angels beside her. She looked up and smiled as I came in, then looked down at Nicky again, and I knew at that point that she was going to live.

'Thanks, Mum. Thank you to all of you,' I said with tears in my eyes. It didn't stop me worrying, though. In my head I knew she'd be fine, but my heart was still racing with anxiety until a couple of days later when the doctors finally told us she had pulled through the immediate danger.

When Nicky regained consciousness, she said she remembered her nana and some other angels round her bed, comforting her. They're still there with her now as she faces the long recovery process and agonising physio sessions that we hope will mean she will be able to walk again in six to eight months' time.

All this has happened while I've been writing this book. It's been a challenging time, as you can imagine, but it has made me feel all the more strongly how important it is to explain to people the ways in which angels can help them and their loved ones, and how you can ask for their help yourself.

Chapter 8

Miracles from the Afterlife

Angel interventions can sometimes be so subtle that it is hard to convince sceptical friends that they happened. The voice you heard in your head could easily be dismissed as 'a vivid imagination' or 'plain common sense'. Avoiding that car accident could just have been 'lucky timing' or 'pure coincidence'. Scientists might argue that the 'strong feeling' you got was based on all sorts of subliminal clues you picked up at the time. *You* know better, of course, but it's frustrating not being believed.

The stories in this last chapter are among the most extraordinary I have come across in all my years of working with spirit. There is no scientific way of explaining the events described here. No matter what your belief system, you have to accept in each of these cases that something beyond our understanding stepped in to save the day. People of different faiths and religions have their own names for 'angels', but no matter what you call them, there is no doubt in all these stories that a spirit or energy force of some sort intervened to help those in mortal danger. Otherwise, they simply wouldn't be alive any more.

Stormy Weather

One of the strangest stories I have come across reminds me of the mariner's tales of old, in which there is a shipwreck and a miraculous rescue. History has written off these tales – such as mermaids saving sailors from drowning after a storm and hauling them onto the shore – as 'fairy stories'. But perhaps they weren't. Perhaps, as in this story I heard from a man called Robert, they were rescued by angels.

My boat was moored at Poole in Dorset and I often sailed solo in the waters of that part of the English Channel, so I knew them well. The forecast had been for calm weather so I took the boat out past the Needles to the west of the Isle of Wight and into the open ocean. Suddenly the wind picked up and it was exhilarating. I was in my element, but at the same time I realised I'd better head for the nearest land in case it got any wilder. I checked my watch – it was 2.30 pm – and started to prepare the sails, but the storm came so fast and so hard I didn't even have time to turn the boat around. A massive wave washed over me, the mast snapped and that's the last thing I remember until I woke up on a deserted sandy beach.

I sat up and clutched my head. There was a huge bump and a bleeding cut on my forehead. I was lying in the hull of the boat but the mast and sails were nowhere in sight. I suppose the mast must have hit me on the head and knocked me unconscious as it fell, but I was incredibly lucky that it hadn't knocked me overboard at the same time. Then I realised that the boat had a gaping hole in the side. How on earth had I made it to dry land without sinking?

All at once I remembered a calm voice talking to me at the height of the storm. It had said 'It's not your time. You still have much to do to help in the world.' I didn't recognise the voice but it sounded male, and I realised it had spoken to me while I lay unconscious, as if in a dream. I'm not a religious person but there was something that felt very odd and spiritual about the experience.

As soon as I felt well enough, I stood and walked up the beach until I found a road. I flagged down a passing driver and asked him where I was.

When he told me, I couldn't believe my ears. That was miles and miles further west than the area where I had been sailing. I must have been unconscious for ages. I checked my watch but it was only 3.05pm – 35 minutes after the storm blew up. Could my watch have stopped? I checked with the driver, and his watch agreed with mine.

Later, when I got home, I pored over my shipping charts. It should have taken at least an hour and a half to get to the beach where I ended up, even with the winds and tide carrying me along, so how had I got there so quickly? I was incredibly lucky that I hadn't been washed up on rocks, because the coastline of Dorset is predominantly rocky, or carried further out into the Atlantic Ocean. And the Channel is so busy that it's a miracle I wasn't hit by one of the big cross-Channel ferries or supertankers that steam along the shipping lanes there.

I thought back to the voice I had heard and realised that the only explanation was that a guardian angel looked after me that day. I also realised that they must have rescued me for a reason and I began to examine my life to try and find out what it is that I am supposed to do. The whole experience changed me and made me look at the world in a different way.

Robert came to see me as part of his search to find his life's purpose. He had a perfectly good job teaching design engineering at university but he realised that he wanted to give more back to the world. He has now begun training as a counsellor and plans to do some voluntary work overseas, bringing comfort to people living in war zones. He is convinced that there was a reason why an angel stepped in to save his life that day – and so am I.

Miracle on a Mountain

Tim has been drawn to mountains since he was a little boy, when his father used to take him for long walks round their home in the Scottish Highlands. When he got to university, he joined a mountaineering club and bought the correct equipment to go on some proper climbs, both in Scotland's famous Munros and in the Alps. He told me he loves the clean, clear air at altitude, the views for miles in all directions, and the feeling of achievement when you reach a summit after hours of exhausting work. He was fully aware of the dangers and always followed proper safety procedures when climbing. But accidents will happen when you are out in the elements, and one day he had a very close shave indeed.

It was a perfect summer day when a friend and I decided to climb a stunning mountain in the Torridon area. We chose a route that involved some rock climbing over the mountain's buttresses. My friend was several feet behind me when suddenly the rock on which I was standing gave way and I fell. There was a sheer drop beneath me at that stage and I remember thinking 'This is it. I'm going to die.'

The fall seemed to happen in slow motion. I'd always thought that if I fell it would be split seconds before I was dashed onto the rocks below so there would be no time to think about it, but this fall seemed leisurely, almost as if something was supporting me on the way down. I watched the rock face going past and the white puffy clouds in blue sky above, and then instead of crashing to the ground, I landed on a ledge I hadn't noticed before. Strangely, there was no impact. It was as if a giant hand gently placed me there.

I looked back up at my friend, at least 30 feet above me, and realised that after falling that distance I should have broken bones at the very least. I sat up and felt my legs first, then my arms. It was a narrow ledge but I managed to stand up and couldn't feel any pain in my back or pelvis. I was a bit dazed, so I sat down again, but otherwise I felt fine.

'Are you OK? Shall I call for help?' my friend was shouting.

'I'm fine,' I yelled back. 'Don't come down. I'll come back up towards you.'

'You sure?' he asked, incredulous. 'You really don't need help?'

We didn't talk about what had happened until we got back down the mountain.

'It was bizarre to watch because you seemed to fall so slowly,' my friend said. 'And it was incredibly lucky that ledge was there. I don't remember seeing it on the way up but it definitely saved your life.'

I didn't want to tell him what I was thinking inside my head. In fact, I've found it difficult to tell anybody since then in case they think I am exaggerating or unhinged in some way, but I have a clear memory of the fall and I'm convinced that someone or something was supporting my body on the way down and they literally placed me on that ledge, thus saving me from serious injury. When I took my clothes off that evening, I didn't have so much as a scratch or a bruise on me. I didn't believe in angels before this happened but I do now.

The fall hasn't stopped me climbing but I take more precautions when there is a steep drop below. I can't rely on angels coming to the rescue every time.

Tim is right: it's up to each of us to take responsibility for our own safety. No matter how much you ask the angels for help, if you keep putting yourself into life-threatening situations then eventually you will get hurt. I don't think the angels were telling him not to climb any more, because it's obvious that he finds climbing a source of great beauty and approaches it in a very spiritual way, but he's had a reminder not to get too complacent.

Underwater Terror

With many outdoor pursuits, you put your trust in another person – perhaps a guide who takes you white water rafting, or the instructor who does your first parachute jump with you. In situations where you are putting your life in someone else's hands, listen hard to your instincts about that person before you start. Ask the angels if it is a good idea. I know Catherine wishes she had stopped to think a bit harder one day during her summer holiday.

A good friend of mine has a brother called Gary who loves scuba diving and while we were on holiday in Cornwall, he persuaded us all to give it a try. He is a trained diving instructor and told us he had a mate who could lend us some scuba equipment.

I felt very nervous at first. Gary is a bit of a loveable rogue and I didn't know his mate from Adam, but they seemed convincingly knowledgeable and everyone else was going along with the plans.

My sister went down for a dive first and came back up full of excitement, saying how incredible it was down there with lots of fish and beautiful rock landscapes. I decided I was being stupid to hesitate. Why not give it a go? I put on the equipment she took off, strapped the tank to my back and placed the mouthpiece in my mouth, then Gary led me out into the water.

The coast shelved very steeply at that point and soon I felt as though we were a long way down from the surface. The underwater world was fantastic, just as my sister had said, with silvery fish darting here and there. Gary was always nearby so I felt very safe. After about ten minutes, he signalled that it was time to go back up and I turned to follow him when suddenly an undercurrent started pulling me away, further out to sea. The ocean began to get darker, so I knew I was going deeper, and then with complete horror I realised I couldn't breathe through my mouthpiece any more. There was no oxygen coming out of it. I gasped as hard as I could several times before panic set in.

'Please God, don't let me die!' I was shouting in my head. 'Help me!'

I heard the words 'Swim up,' and that's what I started to do. The light seemed miles away and I didn't think I was going to make it but then I felt a sensation like hands holding my body and pulling me upwards. I didn't have to try any more because something was lifting me. When my head broke the surface, I took the biggest breath ever, then another, deep into my aching lungs, then I looked around and realised I was a long way away from my friends. They were in the distance, waving and swimming towards me, obviously having realised that something had gone wrong. I floated on my back, getting my strength back and thanking the angels who had saved my life, until they got to me.

Back on shore, Gary examined my equipment to see what had gone wrong and quickly found the problem. A hole in the airline had been patched up with tape that had come loose as I was dragged into the undercurrent.

Thank God for those angels who saved my life. I was in great danger and desperate not to die and they came through for me when I asked.

It's interesting that Catherine felt nervous before she got in the water. I think that was an angel trying to warn her about the danger, but she allowed her fears to be over-ruled in the excitement. It's difficult to be the killjoy when everyone else is having fun, but maybe next time she will think twice.

Alone in the Skies

It must be a fantastic feeling to fly a light aircraft solo – swooping through the skies with vast space all around, underneath and above you. But if something goes wrong, it can be very scary. Pete was an experienced pilot who owned his own plane and frequently flew from Biggin Hill airfield in southeast London to Le Touquet in northern France, just for lunch or a day out. Here's what happened on one occasion that he'll never forget as long as he lives.

I was heading back across the Channel and the mouth of the Thames estuary had just come into view when the words 'High winds' came into my head. The voice was so clear that I thought it must be air traffic control and I radioed them.

'Did you just contact me about high winds?' I asked and told them my flight path.

'No, there are no high winds forecast.' They said I should have a clear run into Biggin Hill that afternoon.

I was flying at low altitude, much lower than commercial aircraft, and certainly the skies looked clear and sunny, the plane was handling smoothly and there was no reason to think anything could go wrong.

About three minutes later, the voice came again, simply saying 'High winds'. It was as clear as if someone was standing in the cockpit behind me. I even turned round to check, but of course there was no one there.

You can get freak winds seemingly coming from nowhere on the clearest of days – it wasn't entirely impossible – so I decided to descend a bit. Just as I began my descent, a fierce tail wind caught the plane so hard that it twisted me right round by 180 degrees, and I ended up facing back in the direction I had come. That had never happened to me before in all my years of flying. I wrestled with the controls to bring the nose up, adrenaline pumping through my veins and sweat standing out on my forehead.

As soon as I could, I contacted air traffic control to tell them what had just happened. 'We've got no other reports of freak winds in that area,' they said, before giving me new instructions for coming in to land.

I looked at my instruments and that's when fear really gripped me: the readings were all completely wrong. They were telling me I was at an impossibly high altitude, which I knew I wasn't, and also that I was tilted way over to the right – yet I could see from the horizon outside that I wasn't. I banged the instrument panel and the needles flickered but didn't right themselves. I would have to bring the plane in to land without using my instruments.

There was a moment when panic took over and I considered strapping on my parachute and bailing out.

But the Thames estuary is a busy area and no matter how hard I tried to steer towards empty space, people down below could still be killed.

'Safe landing,' said the voice in my head, and suddenly I could make out the airfield in the distance.

I got back in touch with air traffic control and told them I was flying without instruments but that I had visuals on the runway. They wanted me to turn and approach from another direction because of a cross wind that had blown up suddenly, but as I tried to execute the turn I realised I no longer had control of my rudder. Something must have been damaged when the tail wind span me round.

'No can do,' I told them. 'I'm coming in straight.' I'd have to tilt the plane at the last minute because when you land in a cross wind you have to balance on one wheel at first instead of trying to land on both. It was going to be extremely hard without instruments. One degree too far over and I'd somersault when I hit the ground.

But at that moment the wind changed again so instead of landing in a cross wind, I was flying into a headwind, which is much easier. All the way, the mysterious voice was giving me directions: 'Tip the nose', 'Ease back on the throttle' and so forth. I touched down and came to a smooth halt just outside the hangar, then I laid my head down on my hands, shaking like a leaf.

When I got out and inspected the bodywork, I nearly collapsed. The damage that had been caused to my tail mechanics should have made it impossible to keep the plane in the air, never mind land. I'm an engineer by profession, and by all the laws of physics as I understand them, that plane should have been uncontrollable. I've always been a black and white person, not given to fancy, but I know for sure something happened in the air that day that can't be explained by science.

Pete's wife is a very spiritual lady who comes to me for readings and she told me about her husband's narrow escape on her next visit. We both agreed there had been angelic intervention that day. I asked if it would stop Pete from flying in future.

'Goodness, no,' she laughed. 'He loves that plane. Nothing would stop him flying.'

I just hope he doesn't start thinking he's invincible and that he will be looked after by angels every time, because it doesn't work like that. He's had a warning.

The Roadside Bomb

In a wartime situation, death is around every corner – literally. Soldiers need to keep their wits about them at all times and use every one of their senses to anticipate danger and react to it in time. John was serving in Basra during the Iraq War, back in the early days after the invasion. He and his colleagues had to do regular patrols in their armoured vehicles on the lookout for insurgents, and this was always a particularly tense part of the day.

We were trundling along in a relatively safe zone of Basra and my mates and I were cracking jokes to relieve the tension when suddenly I heard the word 'Stop!' in my head, as clear as a bell.

'Why?' I asked out loud.

My mates looked at each other and screwed up their faces. 'What are you talking about? Why what?'

'Who said stop?' I asked, but they all told me it hadn't been them, so I decided I'd been imagining things. It's very noisy inside armoured vehicles and sounds from outside can get distorted.

We continued for a while longer and then the voice said 'Stop now!' and it sounded so clear and authoritative that I immediately told our driver to stop, which he did.

'What's that about?' they all asked me. 'Why have we stopped?'

I couldn't give them any explanation, but somehow I just knew we shouldn't go any further at that time. Was there a reason why I'd heard that voice? Maybe we should get out and have a look around, I suggested.

The guys were joking that I was going doolally but we opened the hatch and scanned the surroundings carefully, then three of us got out of the vehicle. While we were standing looking around, another armoured vehicle passed us and continued along the road we'd been on. We checked down a side lane and behind an old shack and were just heading back to our vehicle when there was a huge flash up ahead and then a resounding crack followed by a trail of smoke.

We leapt onboard and drove as fast as we could up the road towards the site of the explosion, where we found that the vehicle that had overtaken us just a minute before had been blown to smithereens by a roadside bomb. The guys inside had all perished.

My first feeling was one of overwhelming guilt. It would have been us killed by that bomb, if it hadn't been for me hearing a voice. I almost felt as though it was my fault those men were dead. I lay on my bed, going over the events again and again, wondering what I could have done differently. Should I have signalled to the other tank to stop as well simply because I heard a voice in my head? Would they have listened to me?

One evening a few days later, when I was agonising about everything for the umpteenth time, my grandad appeared before me. He had died eight years before and

I knew he was a spirit but he seemed just like his old self, smiling at me with his gentle smile.

'A time to live and a time to die,' he said. 'It's your time to live.' Then he disappeared before I could say anything in reply.

I've done a lot of thinking since that time. I wasn't a religious person beforehand but I knew instinctively it must have been an angel who had saved us that day, and after that I started asking the angels for protection every time we went out on patrol. As the months went on, my whole view of the war began to change. I found it wasn't easy to make any sense of the conflict and all the killing that was going on around us and I came to the belief that war never solves anything. What is important in life is to be the best person you can – 'As you sow, so shall you reap' – and not to live in the past but to look forwards, while being grateful for everything we have.

I'm back from Iraq now and full of gratitude for the unseen helpers who looked after me out there. I had other moments of extreme danger during my tour of duty but got out of them using my army skills. It was just that one day when I knew for sure that angels were watching over me. For me – and for the other lads in my vehicle – it was a genuine miracle.

Over the centuries, hundreds of soldiers returning from battle have given accounts of miraculous interventions that have saved lives in ways they were at a loss to explain. Some have described seeing angels, or hearing voices, while others have just been stunned by an escape that didn't seem possible at the time yet somehow happened.

In August 1914, in the first major engagement of the First World War, a British expeditionary force was confronted by several German battalions at Mons. They were greatly outnumbered in both men and firepower and soon found themselves outflanked. Despite suffering heavy casualties, the British soldiers managed to hold back the Germans for several days as they retreated to safety, and stories started to spread that they had been helped by angels. Some wrote that they saw a row of shining beings between the two sides and others saw glowing shapes, but all the accounts, from soldiers who didn't know each other, were remarkably similar. Of course, once these reports were published in the press, they caused huge controversy and experts turned out in force to discredit them as 'hallucinations'. But stories of the angels of Mons continued to spread and recruitment into the British army was vastly increased as a result, because everyone thought that God was obviously on the British side.

Of course, angels don't take sides like this, and they can't save everyone in battle. That's not how it works. But if my son had chosen to serve in the armed forces, I know I would be praying to angels for his safety every single day.

Found in the Rubble

During the Second World War, people back home suffered huge casualties as a result of the bombing of cities, both in Britain and in Germany. There are countless tales of miraculous escapes from collapsing buildings, and of extraordinary bravery. I happen to know a man called Simon who worked as a warden in London, whose job was to search ruined properties after bombing raids and get help for the injured. It was incredibly dangerous work, as buildings could be on fire or severely structurally damaged, but he hadn't been found fit to go out and fight in the army and he felt this was the least he could do for the war effort. Here's a story he told me about an encounter he had one night.

We were working our way down a street where several buildings had been pretty much reduced to rubble. One house had a gaping hole in the side and was leaning ominously.

'Has that one been checked?' I called to my colleague (who was also my boss).

'Yes, it's fine,' he replied.

Suddenly I had an overwhelming urge to check that house for myself. I've got no idea why but my feet just wouldn't let me walk past it.

'Can I have another look, sir?' I requested. He was surprised, but after a moment's hesitation he agreed, telling me to be quick about it.

I climbed carefully up the stairs, listening to the loud creaks the building was making and sniffing carefully in case there was a gas leak. I looked in the front bedroom, where one wall was completely missing, then went through to the back bedroom, but I couldn't see anyone at all. I turned to go back downstairs, but at that point there was a loud voice in my head: 'Under the bed,' it said urgently. 'Under the bed.'

There was a bed upturned against the wall and covered with rubble. I didn't think anyone could possibly be under it but I pulled off some of the heavy stones and lifted the mattress back and underneath there was a piteous sight. Two small children were huddled together with looks of pure terror on their faces that I will never forget as long as I live. I can see them now. There was blood everywhere and they were whimpering softly like terrified animals.

I lifted them out carefully and realised that the little girl's lower arm was virtually severed at the elbow and the wound was bleeding heavily. I needed to get help immediately. I told the little boy to wait, that I would be back for him straight away, and I sprinted down the stairs with her in my arms, then I ran up the street to take her to the ambulance crew I knew were waiting up there. She had lost a lot of blood but I found out later that night that her life had been saved.

When I went back for her brother, he told me their parents had been out and had left their aunt to babysit for them. I went back into the ground floor of the house to look for the aunt and found her body in the kitchen, where she had been killed by falling rubble. That's why the children were all alone. Later that evening, I was able to track down the boy's parents and reunite them, while telling them which hospital their daughter was in.

To this day I don't know what made me look under the bed. I've thought about it often and the only conclusion I can reach is that the children's guardian angel spoke to me. From that point on for the rest of the war, I listened to any voices in my head while I was searching bombed buildings and I found they always gave useful information.

I think a lot of people who work for the emergency services get so used to listening to voices in their heads that they don't think anything of it any more. They have to make decisions quickly in dangerous situations and so they do the first thing that comes into their minds. If they analyse it later, they might explain it away as 'professional instincts' – but in my opinion angels are with these brave people the whole time they are at work. Firemen, ambulancemen, coastguards, policemen and all the other rescue services rely on angels in their day-to-day work and most of them probably don't realise it. But some do …

A Brutal Attack

Those of a nervous disposition might want to skip this story, which was told to me by a policeman called Nigel.

It was a late November evening and I was walking the beat in an inner London district when I heard a blood-curdling scream that made me stop in my tracks.

'Where the hell did that come from?' I asked the colleague who was with me.

'Where did what come from?'

'That scream, of course,' I told him. But he claimed he hadn't heard anything except the noise of our boots on the pavement.

I told myself it might have been a cat howling in a back alley and we carried on, but five minutes later I heard another terrifying scream and this time I was sure it was human because it was followed by a voice saying 'Help her, help her!'

'Help who, and where?' I asked out loud.

'Is that you hearing things again?' my colleague teased. 'I'll have to get the men in white coats to come and lock you up.'

On the other side of the road there was a disused factory. 'It's coming from in there,' I said and hurried across to it. My colleague followed reluctantly, still mocking me.

We found a side door that was slightly ajar and made our way in. All the time, the voice was telling me where to go. 'This way, up the stairs, along here.' Somehow I knew I had to get to the top floor.

When we reached the top, I pushed open a door and nearly threw up at the sight that met my eyes. A young woman had been beaten so badly that she was unrecognisable. She'd been pregnant and the beating had obviously made her go into labour because two tiny babies lay in a pool of blood between her legs, still attached by their umbilical cords.

We called for back-up and went over to try and help her until the ambulance got there. She was semi-conscious but couldn't speak because of a badly broken jaw. I was shaking as I tried to cradle the babies to keep them warm and I knew my colleague was only just holding back his tears. We'd been in the police force for many years and seen some terrible things but that was the most shocking by a long shot.

Several days later, the woman was well enough for me to visit her in hospital and establish what had happened. She told me she had witnessed a robbery and gone to the police to identify the culprits, and that's why they came to get her and beat her up. As well as her broken jaw, she had five broken ribs and a dislocated shoulder, and multiple cuts and bruises all over. The babies were six weeks premature and sadly one was brain-damaged, but the other was fine.

'How did you find me?' she asked.

'I heard you screaming,' I told her.

She looked puzzled. 'But I didn't scream. They told me that if I made a sound, I would die a slow and painful death and they would kill my babies as well. I didn't dare scream.' Then she looked thoughtful. 'While I was lying there, I heard a voice telling me to hold on and that help was coming. "Be strong," it said, "because your babies need you." Even though I was only half-conscious, I knew that I would be found.' She looked at me. 'I don't know what you believe in, but I think that an angel spoke to me and somehow it managed to make you hear screaming as well. That angel saved my life and my babies' too.'

I thought back to all the instructions I'd had from a voice in my head and realised it was the only possible answer. There is no way I would ever have found her on the top floor of that disused factory without divine guidance. It makes me shiver to think about it even now.

Born in a Doss House

Many women have told me about angels who helped them during traumatic childbirth experiences, whether it was the spirit of their mother or grandmother who came to watch over them or another kind of guardian angel they didn't know. But this story is one of the most moving I've ever heard, about a woman called Tracey who was badly down on her luck at the time.

By the time I found out that I was pregnant, the father had already disappeared from the scene. I couldn't bear the thought of an abortion so I decided that I would have the baby and then put it up for adoption. It was hard, though, because my family made it clear they wanted nothing to do with me and the only place I could find to stay was sharing a room with an alcoholic friend in a doss house full of boozers and druggies. I had to sleep on the floor because the place was so crowded, and the atmosphere was awful, with constant fights and arguments. When I was seven months' pregnant, the world seemed such a bleak place that I tried to take my own life one night by cutting my wrists, but although there was a lot of blood, I didn't manage to cut deeply enough to kill myself. I crawled through the next two months in a deep depression, some days too sad to get up and eat a meal.

When I went into labour, the pains came so fast and strong that I couldn't get myself up from the floor, never mind down the stairs and off to hospital. My room-mate was in a drunken stupor and I couldn't rouse her, and although I shouted for help, no one else so much as put their head round the door. The pain was continuous and I felt the urge to push, but I knew that would make the baby come and I was still hoping I could get to hospital somehow.

Suddenly there was a bright light, as if someone had switched on a powerful torch. I got a strange sense that another person was in the room with me, and somehow I knew I was going to be all right. A man appeared by my side with light glowing all around him. I couldn't make out his face clearly but when he touched my forehead the pain eased, and I felt more safe than I had ever felt in my entire life. I don't think he said anything – I was probably making too much noise to hear if he had – but he stayed by my side comforting me as my baby son came into the world.

I reached down to pick up my baby for a cuddle and when I looked up again the man had gone. At that exact moment, there was a knock on the door and an ambulanceman and -woman came in and took over.

'Look's like you've done all the hard work yourself, love,' they said as they cut the cord and wiped the baby down.

'How did you know I was here?' I asked, bemused.

'We got a call saying a woman was giving birth here. Caller didn't give their name but we got here as soon as we could anyway.'

I lay back as they helped me to deliver the placenta. Who could have phoned? There were no phones in the house and none of the other occupants would have been capable of placing the call, even if they had cared enough to try.

When I stood up to make my way to the ambulance, we noticed there were two tiny white feathers on the floor.

The ambulanceman remarked, 'You must have had a guardian angel looking after you today.'

Straight away, I realised that was what had happened, and I thought I knew who it was as well. My Uncle Bill had died many years before but he had always been very good to me when I was a little girl. As soon as I had the thought, I knew instinctively that it was true. Uncle Bill had been with me as I gave birth.

'I'm going to call the baby William,' I told the ambulanceman.

After such a miraculous birth, there was no way I could bear to give up my little boy for adoption. I didn't want to be parted from him ever. I applied to the council and they gave us a lovely council flat, the first place in my life that has ever truly felt like a home. William and I are very safe and settled there, and I know that Uncle Bill still watches over us.

When I last heard from Tracey, she and William were doing very well. She has a job she enjoys and is proving to be a fantastic mother. She had to suffer to get where she is now, but maybe that was all part of her life plan and has made her a better person today.

Learning to Listen

I hope that the stories in this book have helped you to think about your own experiences and that in future you will always listen to your own voices. Every one of us is psychic to an extent and it is a gift that can be developed with practice. Only a few of us can communicate with spirit clearly enough to work as a psychic medium but that doesn't mean that you can't enhance your life immeasurably by paying attention to your angels and asking them for help when you're in trouble.

If you would like to tell me your own angel stories, or perhaps attend one of my seminars, you can get in touch via my website www.dorothychitty.co.uk. I'd love to hear from you.

The thought I would like to leave you with is that you are NEVER ALONE. There's always someone with you: taking care of you, warning you if need be. You need to learn to ask and believe you will be helped. Be precise and clear in what you're asking, both for yourself and for others, and you will be heard.

Love and blessings to you,

Dorothy

Acknowledgements

I would like to thank:

all my friends and clients who have so generously shared their stories with me, enabling this book to be written;

Michael, my dear husband, for his endless support, encouragement and love;

my three children Carl, Nicky and Tanya, and also Mark my son-in-law, who listened to the stories with open minds and sometimes open mouths; with their helpful suggestions, they helped keep my feet on the ground;

my good friend Jan Cload for helping me type up the stories at the very beginning, Katy Carrington for suggesting I write this book and last, but by no means least, the two gifted women, Gill Paul and my editor Susanna Abbott, for their support and creative input throughout the writing of this book.

what's next?

Tell us the name of an author you love

Dorothy Chitty | Go

and we'll find your next great book